DISCOVER JAPAN Vol. 1

Words, Customs and Concepts

KODANSHA INTERNATIONAL

Tokyo and New York

Front cover photo: Lacquerware by Yamaka
Back cover photo: Model food by Sudo

Previously published in 1975 by the Japan Culture Institute
as *A Hundred Things Japanese*, ISBN 0-87040-364-8.

Distributed in the United States by Kodansha Internation-
al/USA Ltd., 114 Fifth Avenue, New York, New York 10011.
Published by Kodansha International Ltd., 17-14, Otowa
1-chome, Bunkyo-ku, Tokyo 112 and Kodansha Interna-
tional/USA Ltd.
LCC 82-48294
ISBN 0-87011-835-8
ISBN 4-7700-1335-3 (in Japan)

First edition, 1982
This edition, 1987
Fourth printing, 1990

PREFACE

The Japanese are inveterate list-makers. Lists are considered informative all by themselves and many are the publications which consist of merely such. Merely, one says, and yet is not listing the first and most important step toward understanding? Unless one knows all the ingredients that contribute toward the creation of a form, will one ever understand this form? And without an understanding of form, will one ever discover its function?

It was such considerations that led the compilers of this present collection of words, customs and concepts to see that one of the ways of beginning to understand Japan was to imitate this basic learning process and list things about the country and the people.

This listing is arbitrary—one might say carefully arbitrary. Since any ordering of parts comes after their listing, there is no reason to attempt any preliminary editing. Indeed, there is considerable reason not to. In an arbitrary listing there is, in truly Japanese fashion, an accurate reflection of the variety and vitality of the things listed. A cornucopia is discovered, and this lack of order becomes a reflection of the promise and prodigality of an entire culture.

At the same time a very loose plan has been imposed. Since the ingredients are all Japanese, a Japanese grid was thought fitting. The paradigm is very Japanese—the seasons: the seasons of the year, the seasons of life. Thus, New Year's customs, things concerning childhood, etc., are toward the front of the book; those concerning *Kurisumasu* (Christmas), old age, etc., are listed toward the end.

Other stipulations have also been observed. For example, all the entries are by foreigners—people in Japan but not themselves

Japanese. This is because Japanese writers take too much for granted: it is, after all, their culture. Foreigners living in Japan take nothing for granted: everything must be examined and then placed, correctly it is hoped, in the context of Japanese life. A further imposition was that these foreign writers were encouraged to be as personal as they wished. Though famous scholars of things Japanese were included along with rank new Japan hands, all were asked to give personal reactions along with their accurate objective descriptions. Such an amount of information, mixed with opinion and prejudice, would, it was felt, give all these things Japanese a lively context of their own—a volume within the volume.

Finally, it will be noticed that this arbitrary-within-limits quality (a very Japanese one) has the added advantage of providing a kind of indirection. To present a living country and culture through the facets of unordered things is neither quixotic nor impractical. Facets reflect the light, they also reflect the shape of the thing itself. Perhaps it is, indeed, only in this indirect way that the complexity and complications of a culture can be truly suggested.

DONALD RICHIE
1982

Japanese words in this book are spelled according to the modified Hepburn system and printed in italics the first time they appear, except for those words that have entered the English vocabulary and thus are listed in *Webster's New World Dictionary*. Japanese names are printed in the Japanese order, family name first.

Many thanks are due to Clifton Karhu for the ink drawings, and to all of those whose photographs are used; to the editors and publications that furnished other illustrations; and, of course, to the many foreign contributors who made this book possible.

Hatsu-môde, 初詣

The first shrine or temple visit, made during the New Year.

The New Year holiday season is called *O-shôgatsu* in Japan. It is, without a doubt, the most universally and enthusiastically celebrated of all the numerous festivities in the Japanese calendar.

Toward the end of December, the traditional pine and bamboo decoration (*kado-matsu*) begins to appear at the entrance to everything that can be called a building. As the year draws nearer to its closing hours, everyone scurries about, laying away provisions for those first three days of the new year when there is literally nothing open anywhere.

Then on the eve of the year to come, shortly after eleven, hoards of people begin swarming into shrine or temple precincts all over the country, to be the very first to pay their respects, to clap their hands to call the attention of all the gods to themselves, to toss their coins into the offering bins, and to buy their arrows, votive tablets, and talismans, for the best possible health and good fortune during the next three hundred sixty-five days.

Those who choose not to brave the cold, the crowds, and the all-night trains of New Year's Eve can take advantage of their long vacation to visit their favorite shrine or temple at their leisure, until about January 7th. And this they do in crowds that never seem to end. Thus this first shrine visiting (*hatsu-môde*) is the most conspicuous of the many Japanese New Year customs.

During my fifteen years of residence in this lovely land, I have fallen into the habit of joining these "first night" crowds, and faithfully buy my very own lucky arrow each year. I never actually decided to get into this particular habit, it just sort of infiltrated itself into my life. Thus as the year comes to a close, I always find myself making plans for either the grand tour of Kamakura's Tsurugaoka Hachiman Shrine at midnight and around to Enoshima for sunrise, or the shorter jaunt to Meiji

Shrine and back home quickly to sleep through the first dawn of the new year.

I did not realize just how much of a habit it had become, until this year, when, for some reason or other, I did not make my regular pilgrimage, and I found that, as a result, this year seems to have taken a rather longer time than usual to get in the groove of good fortune for me. At any rate, my New Year's resolution for this year is not to miss my shrine visit on the next New Year's Eve.

Don Kenny

O-shôgatsu, お 正 月
The New Year; New Year's Day.
(The "o" is honorific.)

O-shôgatsu, New Year's, is Japan's most important holiday. It is equivalent to our Christmas, being a family day of quiet with presents for the children——usually in the form of *o-toshidama*, a bit of spending money. It is also equivalent to our birthdays since most Japanese, no matter what month they were born, consider themselves a year older after January first.

It is also, like our holidays, a day of eating and drinking. My Japanese wife is at work days before preparing the various delicacies for the main New Year's meal, which is breakfast extending into a leisurely brunch. This is also the single day when I can prevail on her not to do the housecleaning, and it is certainly the only day of the year when she will willingly wear that most attractive of costumes, the traditional Japanese kimono.

On the night before, my family and I have been to the local shrine and, after five New Year's here, I pray for coming good fortune just as hard as any of my neighbors. Then, at midnight, we listen for the one hundred eight bells which signal the passing of the old year.

The day itself I spend, replete with good food——including the traditional baked rice cakes, *mochi*, and the even more traditional sake——in front of the television set. This is not so odd as it sounds and many Japanese do the same. The reason is that the day's programs themselves constitute a celebration featuring the traditional performing arts of Japan.

After that, it is time to read all the greeting cards that the postman has brought. The charming custom is to send best wishes to friends and acquaintances and the more you get (or send) the more popular you are. I am by now Japanese enough to have this urge to send cards even to people I really don't much like, hoping we will be friends during the New Year.

The cards keep coming for several days because the New Year's season is spread out over a week. Indeed, if you do not shop before the holidays you will have nothing to cook because all the stores will be closed for at least the first few days. The Japanese work right up to midnight of the day before, getting all duties done, paying back all debts, collecting all money due.

Then on the day itself, by yourself or with your family, you can start the New Year properly, the slate rubbed clean, a full, new, empty and promising year in front of you. Everyone makes lots of resolutions, plans are made, diaries are begun. In Japan the New Year is really what the phrase implies—a renewal. Thus one can't help feeling a new amount of strength and hope upon hearing the common greeting: *Akemashite omedetô gozaimasu* . . . The very best wishes upon the opening of the New Year.

Jack Walraven

Hari-kuyô, 針 供 養

A "needle mass," i.e. a requiem
service for broken needles.

February 8 is the day of *hari-kuyô*, when Buddhist masses are
sung for needles broken during the past year, as it is considered
that the needles' lives were sacrificed in service. After all,
without the clever, subtle needle clothes could not be mended
or kimono resewn as they must be after each washing. This
ceremony is particularly popular in girls' schools.

A little three-step altar is set up and hung with a sacred rope
and the strips of cut white paper associated with sanctified
places. On the top step of the altar are arranged offerings of

fruit and sweet cakes. On the middle step is placed a cake of *tôfu* (white solidified bean curd); and on the bottom step are arranged various sewing accessories, such as scissors and threads and thimbles. The tôfu makes a soft cool cushion wherein the unfortunate broken needles can be set to rest. It is a soothing place for the needles to live in comfortably after their days of hard service. To give the needles spiritual comfort and to calm their hurt spirits sutras are sung, especially in Buddhist schools.

In Tokyo, this cake of tôfu containing pieces of needles is then brought to a shrine, in a ceremony particularly beloved by dressmakers and those proud of their needlework. Although the origins of this interesting custom are not clear, it is said that bringing broken needles to the Kada Shrine (popularly called "Awashima-sama") in Wakayama is auspicious, this shrine being dedicated to the ancient god of medicine. Awashima-sama is also enshrined in Sensô-ji in Tokyo's Asakusa, and a great needle-mass is held annually. It is here that the visitor can most easily observe this charming custom.

It is perhaps not so surprising that needles can be considered living things. In the hands of a skillful seamstress, needles fly so, they must seem to have a life of their own. Furthermore, needles differ from one another in their strength or fineness, almost as people do. And in the days before mass manufacture, the making of fine needles was a difficult skill to which the craftsman gave his best effort, so that some of his soul, in a sense, entered into the needles he made. Furthermore, if broken needles are carefully set aside to be honored, they will not be allowed to go astray in the tatami matting and perhaps hurt someone.

Mary Evans Richie

Hinamatsuri, 雛　祭
Doll Festival, or Girls' Day, falling
on March 3.

Little Japanese girls very often look like perfect dolls, but
rarely do perfect Japanese dolls (painted with mature-looking
faces and living in glass cases because they are much too fragile
and expensive to be handled) look like little girls. There is a
certain irony in the fact that March 3, the day of *Hinamatsuri*
(Doll Festival), should also be Girls' Day in Japan——presumably
the day for honoring the girlishness in girls——for at the focus
of attention on this day are dolls so splendid that no one would
dream of playing with them.

On March 3, girls dress up and invite their friends over to
partake of special refreshments and to admire the doll collection
scrupulously laid out on stepped shelves. The dolls inhabit a
glittering world of miniature food and furniture. Unlike those of
lesser magnificence, these dolls demand not love but awe and
have about them an air of the sacred and the mysterious.

A set of dolls——usually about fifteen when complete
——comprises an emperor, an empress, and their retinue, all
exquisitely attired. Bought today in a department store, sets can
cost upwards of two or three hundred thousand yen, and those
handed down as heirlooms may be priceless. The sets include an
intricate array of paraphernalia: chests of drawers the size of
matchboxes, musical instruments, tables set with sweetmeats, an
orange and cherry tree——even a bullock-drawn carriage. Once I
saw a little lacquer sewing machine inventively constructed in
the way that Lady Murasaki's sewing machine might have been
made, had sewing machines been invented in the Heian period
(794-1185).

In the old days, dolls and furniture were added to the collection when a girl was born into the family, and when a girl
married, she would take her own portion of the collection with
her and add to it when a girl was born to her. After being on
display for about two weeks or so the dolls are carefully put
away, with the other family treasures.

Hinamatsuri has its origins in the ancient practice of ritual purification, in which people breathed their sins onto paper dolls and threw the dolls into the river, and in the custom of picnicking outdoors in the spring. It was in the Edo period (1603-1867) that the dolls came to be modelled after courtiers. Curiously, the Doll Festival reached its pinnacle of popularity during this period, a time when the status of women in Japan had reached its lowest ebb. Hinamatsuri was the one occasion when a girl felt important: this was her festival, she invited the boys, she played the role of hostess.

Angela Carter

Sakura, 桜
The Japanese cherry tree
or its blossoms.

Fifty-one weeks out of the year, the cherry tree receives small notice. A homely tree of average height with plain bark and leaves, it lacks the pine's grandeur, the plum's dignity, the willow's grace. Yet the tree's blossoms, for the one week in spring that they are in bloom, so well suit the Japanese sensibility that the word for flower (*hana*) has become synonymous with them.

In the same botanical family as the rose, the small, scentless *sakura* pales before the fragrant, sensuous petals of its distant cousin. The sakura is a poet's flower, not a painter's: isolated on the artist's canvas it wants the proud distinction of the peony, the camellia, or the chrysanthemum; but isolated in brief verse it harbors emotional overtones that reverberate eternally in the Japanese soul.

The faintly pink petals of a single cherry blossom are a study in solitude, as is a single Japanese; but blooming in profusion the pale blossoms, like the Japanese together, come to life and dominate the landscape. One tree with its myriad blossoms is a pretty sight, but row upon row of trees lining castle moats, river banks, levees and lawns is a spectacle. The Japanese lose themselves in the collective brilliance of the sakura, and when they gather together in lively circles beneath the blossoms, their inhibitions melt away. They drink and sing and dance; they holler and brawl and utter belly laughs. Following the lead of the cherry blossoms, they give themselves over once in the year to effusive, meteoric merriment.

Lurking amid the blossoms' garish beauty, however, is the haunting theme of impermanence——the poetry without which the sakura would never have so completely captivated the hearts of Japanese. No sooner do they reach their peak of efflorescence than the blossoms fall, shaken by a capricious gust, scattered by a chilly spring rain. They fall mercifully, sadly, eloquently: mercifully, because more than a few days of cherry blossom-

viewing would be exhausting; sadly, because the scattering petals traditionally call to mind those whose lives have been cut short; eloquently, because the short-lived blossoms affirm most profoundly the Japanese aesthetic: that what is beautiful in nature and in human life rarely lasts, that evanescence itself is a thing of beauty, and that nostalgic memories of what has fallen at the height of glory are the most beautiful of all.

Edward Fowler

Take, 竹
——Bamboo.

To many Westerners, the very word "bamboo" conjures up a vision of a mystical, exotic plant. On hearing that it can grow to fantastic heights in a matter of days, many are inclined to dismiss this as part of the legend, and equate it with the wondrous happenings of bamboo as related in the classic Japanese fairytale, *Taketori Monogatari*, or "The Bamboo Cutter." I must admit that until I saw a shoot grow rapidly with my own eyes in my garden in Tokyo (six feet in one week), I wasn't ready to believe that part of the legend myself.

However, now having lived in Japan for some time, I realize that it really isn't exotic at all, but in fact, is a plant that plays a very important part in the life of every Japanese. Some learned studies on bamboo list 1,400 uses for this amazing material, but one doesn't have to be learned to think of at least a dozen. Some of the things that come to mind are the chopsticks with which people eat their daily food, and——in the form of bamboo shoots——a foodstuff itself. As one looks around a Japanese home, many other things will be apparent——baskets, placemats, brooms, fans, vases.

To me, the most interesting aspect of bamboo is its resiliency and, in this respect, it reminds me of many traits of the Japanese people. Bamboo is very strong and at the same time very flexible. Because of this, it can be bent, stretched, and pushed into all sorts of shapes, but when it is released, it snaps back to its original form and continues to grow tall and strong. How like the Japanese, who on emerging from a disastrous War, have recovered and forged ahead to become a strong and powerful nation.

Because Japanese and their culture are little known in other parts of the world, they are often regarded as being exotic in the same way as bamboo. But when we look closely we will find that, just like the plant, they are understandable and not inscrutable at all.

Norman H. Tolman

Koinobori, 鯉のぼり
Carp-shaped streamers traditionally
flown on Boys' Day.

The first spring after Japan's surrender was, for this confused
young American in the devastated land of the late enemy,
startlingly beautiful. From the early-blooming plums through a
succession of nature's fireworks, the bright splotches of color on
the dull landscape looked to be ingenuously devised. The climax
came with the *koinobori*——fancifully colorful streamers of cloth
or paper fish undulating in the warm air. I knew then that Japan
would survive the defeat.

Of course, hope and optimism were values that I ascribed to
the delightful pennants which people raised on bamboo poles in
their gardens. Recognizing that they were not really more
blossoms, a Westerner would think perhaps of flags. But in the
shape of ballooning fish?

Explanations were forthcoming. The fish was the carp and each
streamer was for a male child in the house, up to fifteen feet
in length for the eldest and, running down the pole, propor-
tionally smaller ones for the younger. It was a way of celebrating Boys' Day, the fifth day of the fifth month. When I asked
why the carp the answer given was that it was a fish of manly
virtues.

Good enough. Besides, in this form at least, it was bright and
playful, showing a sensitivity to children's taste. No evil could
conceivably be attached to such a lovely custom.

We go through phases in our appreciation of things Japanese,
though, and so in due time I had to take note that manly
virtues could mean militarist virtues. The carp was chosen for its
fearless courage; it swam up waterfalls and when laid out on the
carving board it accepted the fate of the knife without flinching.
Many stories were told, like the one of how carp allied themselves with the Empress Jingû's invasion fleet against the
Koreans. Shrines to the war god Hachiman distributed carp
amulets.

However, another phase was marked with a discovery that

turned the koinobori's symbolism completely around. The custom proved, according to my reading, to have been conceived in the 17th century by city commoners as a clever play upon the samurai's practice of displaying swords and armor on Boys' Day. This was perfect——it rationalized the koinobori as quite befitting a peace-loving Japan.

All of which is undoubtedly beside the point so far as the Japanese are concerned. Nowadays I hear there are even families that hoist koinobori for their daughters! After all, Boys' Day has become Children's Day on the calendar. And this is the last in a string of holidays that the recreation-bent Japanese of the modern era enjoy as "Golden Week." The koinobori endures nicely in such a context.

Holloway Brown

Taue, 田　植
―― Rice transplanting.

Just as rice is the staff of Japanese life, so the manner and customs of rice-planting and harvesting remain at the heart of this island society. *Taue* means literally, to put rice in the field, i.e., to transplant the seedlings from the beds to their prepared fields, heavily irrigated squares of paddies. But over the centuries it came to have vast social meanings. Wet rice farmers live worlds apart from the traditional Western dry farmers of wheat and potatoes. Where labor in one is periodic, labor in the other is unremitting. Above all, where the European farmer could live within his own world of sun, wind and rain, the Japanese farmer needed often complex systems of irrigation to harvest his crop. The Western farmer (not to mention his herdsman ancestors) could afford to be a rugged individualist. The Japanese could not. Irrigation meant cooperation.

Japan is today, on its face, one of the most urban of countries. Yet, economic giantism, technological marvels, networks of mass transport and communication notwithstanding, its society still keeps close to the village society of old Japan. Japanese organize their cities like congeries of small villages. The widely discussed company loyalties of Japanese workers and businessmen come from the same basic sense of being villagers, an instinct so strong that it can impose itself on machines and organizations which were originally devised by other societies, operating on far different premises. The rite of taue is at the heart of this villager's instinct in the Japanese.

Taue imposed its customs and organizations over the centuries. Wet-rice farming, particularly in the narrow plains of Japan, hedged by mountain and sea, began and continued as patchworks of small plots, each surrounded by its steep earth walls and watered by common systems of irrigation. Water was too precious to allow its control to slip away into the hands of individuals or impersonal institutions. The people of Japan devised their own interlocking system of neighborhood respon-

sibilities to channel the water. And society grew around them.

Households established subsidiaries, villages grew and subdivided, complex codes and organizations developed from the needs of this group work. Great modifications have taken place, but their essence has not changed much. The ceremonial rites of Japanese business, not to mention its exasperating fondness ·for complex organization, have deep roots. As the company chairman, surrounded by the massed directors, departments and foot-soldiery of the corporation, offers a toast for the past year's business activities, is he far removed from the *oyakata* of a farming community, handing out the ceremonial rice-cakes and sake at the *Taue-gyôji* of a half-vanished countryside? Perhaps the analogy should not be carried too far. But the hold of taue on Japan's society can not be dismissed. If the modern Japanese can still be called a nation of villagers, their rice culture has made and kept them so.

Frank Gibney

Tanabata, 七　夕

Festival held on the 7th day of
7th month of lunar calendar.

Tanabata is unique among Japanese festivals in its celebration of love. Legend has it that two stars, known as the Cowherd (Altair) and the Weaver (Vega) were lovers separated by the Milky Way and able to meet but once a year, on July 7, if it did not rain.

As the day of the festival drew near, people in an earlier age would gaze nervously at the summer sky and pray for fair weather, offering sweets and food to the stellar lovers. Members of the family wrote auspicious poems on strips of colored paper and decorated bamboo cuttings in the garden with them, in much the same fashion as Westerners decorate a Christmas tree. Young girls believed that by observing the rites of the festival they could improve their skill at weaving, a most important task for a woman in rural Japan, and they prayed to the Weaver Star for guidance. Few women do any weaving nowadays, however, and people more commonly celebrate the festival to improve their calligraphy.

Although the Tanabata legend is of Chinese origin, we can see clearly in it the face of Japan. In an age when arranged marriage was the norm and love matches were frowned upon, the story of two stars meeting once a year if lucky surely appealed to this people's romantic sentiments. And since even today frustrated love affairs are not uncommon, it seems quite natural to conclude that the continued popularity of the festival owes not simply to the Japanese love of pageantry but also to the intensely sentimental side of the Japanese character.

More recently, Tanabata has become symbolic of Japan's estrangement from nature and the simple life. The festival is disappearing from the cities. Bamboo does not grow on asphalt, and few people have gardens in which to decorate the cuttings anyway. Most Japanese nowadays associate Tanabata with Sendai, where each year the festival grows more spectacular and draws more tourists. Those who do not make the pilgrimage are content to sit in their air-conditioned living rooms and, rather than turn their gazes heavenward, watch the spectacle on television.

Glenn Davis

Matsuri, 祭
A festival, a fête, a feast.

Recently I dug up some old notes scribbled in a diary after I had attended my first *matsuri* almost fifteen years ago. I had just arrived in Japan, and went with some friends to the annual festival of the Hachiman Shrine in Kamakura. My diary notes are sketchy, but still I don't have any trouble recalling the combination of wonder and exhilaration I experienced that day, because the same feeling has been repeated many times during the last fifteen years.

Carnivals and street fairs were not new to me, nor were outdoor religious festivals and processions. But the mixture of the sacred and the profane, the solemn and the earthy, rich symbolism and gaudy hucksterism——this was something I had not experienced before. I had the feeling that if one could understand the spirit of the matsuri, then one would have gone a long way toward understanding the Japanese way of looking at the world.

I have long since given up trying to characterize "the Japanese mind," but I still enjoy going to shrine festivals. Recently I attended the Night Festival at Chichibu, on the outskirts of Tokyo, one of the most colorful matsuri in all of Japan. All the elements were there that make the matsuri an exciting event: expectant crowds of people gradually becoming more and more involved in the action; the ceaseless rhythm of drums, flutes and jingling, bell-like instruments; the wild procession of *mikoshi*, or "temporary dwelling places of the gods," weaving in and out through the crowds.

What makes the Chichibu festival particularly colorful is the brightness radiating from the hundreds of lanterns strung around the mikoshi, in this case large, three-tiered floats which have to be pulled by several men with long, sturdy ropes. The stalwart young (and not so young) men pulling the floats and riding on them showed more than the usual degree of "divine intoxication" expected of mikoshi bearers, with sake and contagious enthusiasm providing most of the intoxication. As a background for all this, the winter sky was lit up constantly by a spectacular fireworks display that continued through the evening.

I thought again of how appropriate it was that Abe Kôbô used the "eternal festival procession" as a symbol for the truly authentic life in his novel *The Ruined Map*. The matsuri is one of the best symbols I know of a joyous, free affirmation of life: a world where civilization and spontaneity meet, with people coming together to celebrate life and the mystery of things.

William Currie

**Saijiki,
歳 時 記**
A reference
book of the
seasons.

In every country of the temperate zone the four seasons are distinguished by name, by their agricultural activities, and by their poetic associations. In Japan, however, the emphasis on the seasons in all forms of artistic expression goes far beyond what is considered necessary elsewhere. In what other country, for example, are plays classified according to season? Indeed, works in the Noh repertory are not only designated as "spring" or "summer" plays, but as belonging to "early spring," "mid-spring," or "late spring." Even long Kabuki plays whose action extends over several seasons are generally performed at a particular time of year; *Chûshingura* is most often given in the winter, presumably because the final vendetta scene occurs in the snow.

The seasons were closely reflected by Japanese poetry. The imperial anthologies of tanka opened with six books of seasonal poems, and the order in which they were arranged corresponded exactly to the order in which the events described——the appearance of the first haze, the blossoming of a tree, the song of a bird——would be perceived. Poems about plum blossoms therefore invariably preceded those about cherry blossoms, observing the natural order.

Of all the Japanese poetic forms, the haiku most depends on the season. A haiku without a seasonal word is dismissed as a "miscellaneous" poem of minor importance. Sometimes the season is straightforwardly named, as in "spring sea" or "summer night," but more commonly the seasonal references are indirect. The mention of a plant associated with a particular season is a preferred way of designating a season; not only is it important in a poem of only seventeen syllables not to waste any in specifying the season, but the blossoming of a flower is a more precise indication of the time of year than the bare mention of a season.

Flowers, however, are not the only seasonal indicators. The moon, though visible of course at other times of year, is a designator for autumn, when it appears to greatest advantage; if a haiku poet wants to describe a moonlit night in spring he has to state that it is a "spring moon" to avoid confusion. So many seasonal words were recognized by the late eighteenth century that special books called *saijiki* ("Records of Years and Seasons") were compiled for the guidance of haiku poets. A glance at a saijiki informed the poet, for example, that grasshoppers and wild geese should be mentioned in an autumn verse, but that plovers and wild ducks belonged in a winter one.

The seasons of the saijiki were those of the lunar calendar. When the solar calendar was adopted in 1873 these seasons no longer corresponded to Nature. At New Year, according to the old calendar, one should see the first haze of spring, but when New Year came on January first there was nothing remotely springlike about the scene. It became necessary to invent new saijiki for the haiku poets. Old or new, the existence of such books is a sign of the extraordinary importance that the Japanese of past and present have attached to the seasons.

Donald Keene

Formal kimono, by Miyata Zenjirô

Kimono, き も の
Japanese clothing, specifically,
the robe-like outer garment.

On New Year's Day at any shrine in Japan, there is always a
bevy of young ladies turned out in their finery——colorful new
kimono with sleeves trailing nearly to the ground. Their kimono
show all the colors of the rainbow and some it seems were
invented for young ladies alone.

Color is the only distinguishing feature of the kimono in this
context. They are made nearly all the same size, style and cut
for all wearers regardless of individual differences. When shopping for material for a kimono, one doesn't worry about the
amount of material necessary, since it is already cut and rolled
into standard lengths. The only consideration the buyer need
make is quality and color.

Young ladies used to study the technique of kimono-making

in school as a part of preparation for their role as homemakers. Young ladies of today no longer study the kimono in school but there are many places which offer kimono-making as an evening course. Here young ladies learn the formulas which govern the angles at which collars are cut or the length a sleeve should be made for a certain type of kimono. They also study the art of wearing as well as the art of making the kimono.

Wearing a kimono is not an easy thing. There is the under-kimono, the outer-kimono, and seemingly endless belts and straps which hold each part in position. Putting all of these things in their proper places is a big job for one person and sometimes calls for assistance. In the case of the bridal kimono, the preparations usually require not only a couple of assistants to fit the kimono and its various parts, but also a hair stylist, and a make-up artist, not to mention the bride herself. It is a very colorful experience to watch a wedding party gathering around for the photographs. The bride is clad in a dazzling array of reds and whites all artfully arranged for the best effect while the young unmarried ladies bloom in parti-colored kimono of all hues. Their mothers and older married sisters show off their black formal kimono with designs in gold, silver and white decorating the portion below the obi. Also marking these formal kimono are five *mon* (crests) worked in white: one on the back between the shoulder blades, one on the back of each sleeve and two on the breast.

But not all kimono are so stiff and complicated. In summer, and at the hot springs, the standard garb is the yukata (a light kimono). It is usually in some pattern of blue worked on a white background. It is a light-colored and comfortably cool garment for those hot, humid summer evenings, or while sipping an icy cold beer after enjoying the delights of a soak in a hot springs bath.

Of all the types of kimono, however, my favourite is the flannel winter *nemaki* (sleeping kimono) made for me by my mother-in-law. On a cold winter morning while waiting for the room to warm, short of jumping back under the futon that kimono does the best job of keeping out the cold.

Daniel L. Gossman

Fundoshi, ふんどし

A loincloth, a waistcloth, a breech-cloth.

Whatever its presumed old-fashioned impracticality, and consequent present unpopularity, the *fundoshi* remains an article of clothing eminently suited to human needs and aspirations.

It covers the sex with decency but is not prudish; the tightly tied *rokushaku fundoshi* displays as much as it covers and well reflects traditional male pride. Further, it always gives support. Even the shorter *etchû fundoshi*——an invention of the economy-minded Japanese Army during the Meiji period (1868—

1912)——is designed to support. Further, the supporting function of the fundoshi is flexible. While relaxing or amusing himself the wearer may loosen the garment; on the other hand (and traces of this remain in the phrase *fundoshi o shimenaosu*, meaning to gird one's loins) when going into battle or other exacting action, the wearer can tighten his pouch and prepare himself. The fundoshi is thus indicative of a certain attitude, that of the whole man who rightly considers his sex a part of himself and neither hides nor flaunts it.

How different the apparent attitude of the contemporary wearers of the Western-style *buriifu* or *panti*. When new its supporting function is limited to too tight; after several washings, however, this article ceases to give any support whatever. Its decorative function is nil and it is an encumbrance to all natural functions. The sex of these wearers must seem comparative strangers, to be met with only furtively in bathroom or in bed.

And yet this impractical foreign garment now boasts a far greater number of Japanese wearers than does the fundoshi. That traditional article is a legacy of the South Seas, of Southeast Asia, areas where men unselfconsciously think of themselves as whole and natural. Japan once had this quality. The striking lack of the fundoshi on the contemporary scene is one of several indications that this is no longer so.

Donald Richie

Obi, お び

A length of cloth used as sash
or belt with kimono.

In 1886, Basil Hall Chamberlain tells us (and he was in Japan at the time), shoes, dresses, and corsets were ordered from Berlin so that the ladies of the Japanese Court might cut splendid European figures. "Every foreigner of taste," wrote Chamberlain, attempted to dissuade the Japanese from this folly, and Mrs. Cleveland, wife of the American president, wrote warning the women of the dangers of tight lacing. Within three years that experiment with Western dress was abandoned, but not, presumably, because of the evils of tight lacing. A proper and properly-worn obi was and is as constricting as any nineteenth-century German corset, but the discomfort of the obi, the inordinate time required to put it and the rest of the costume on, the resulting restriction of mobility, were thought, until recently, to be justified by the final elegant effect. The effect, in fact, is found no where else in the history of costume. A sash around the waist seems universal (and may determine, according to the whims of fashion, where the waist is that year), but the obi is much more substantial and serves additional functions.

It is heavy embroidered or brocaded material, about a foot wide and some seven or eight feet long, covering all areas that can possibly be defined as waist. That this chief feminine decoration should encase the center of the body probably follows logically the conception that the midriff is the center of being: in Japanese you don't make up your mind, your belly decides; if your belly's big, you're broad-minded. Obviously, this sensitive, decision-making area requires protection (disease is warded off by wearing a belly-band) and deserves adornment.

The obi, like the flower arrangement, notes the seasons, marks the passage of time. In earliest spring it may display the plum blossom, in midsummer the cooling effect of a mountain stream, in autumn the burning maples, in winter the pine, tenaciously green. And it also changes with the age of the wearer. As a child she wears bright, even, gaudy greens, reds, blues, as a young woman the quieter pastel shades. For the mother the colors fade, for the grandmother they darken to a somber glow. Throughout her life the form of her obi, and kimono, is fixed, only color and texture changing as time passes. The costume is traditional, a form of permanent beauty.

Earle Ernst

Karakasa, からかさ
——An oiled-paper umbrella.

I own a Japanese umbrella. It is a beautiful item with oiled paper and fine bamboo work, brightly colored, lightweight, and perfectly efficient for keeping off both sun and rain. The funny thing is that I use this umbrella in the United States, not in Japan. In the United States it seems exotic, but in Japan it just seems out of place. This is ironic, for the Japanese have used umbrellas for more than a thousand years and have produced parasols which are more than just another form of protection from the weather, they are works of art in their own right.

The Japanese umbrella or parasol is called *karakasa*, which means Chinese umbrella. As the name indicates, at some time in the remote past umbrellas were introduced to Japan from abroad. One of the earliest wall paintings in a prehistoric tomb depicts a nobleman escorted by servants who shelter him with an umbrella. In the eleventh century we find the court lady Sei Shônagon listing karakasa as one of the items essential in every household.

The earliest umbrellas were covered with cloth, usually silk, and they could not be closed. They were used not so much for protection from the rain or sun, but rather as a status symbol by the nobility and the Buddhist clergy, and were patterned with rich designs and often emblazoned with the owner's family crest. The first umbrella which could be opened and closed freely was said to have been imported toward the end of the sixteenth century.

In the Edo period it was refined into something more beautiful and elaborate. Umbrellas made by skilled craftsmen came into wide use by the common people. Until after the end of WW II the streets were enlivened by these umbrellas on rainy days. Unemployed workers eked out a living making them despite the popularity of mass-produced Western umbrellas which had been introduced to Japan in the early Meiji period.

The traditional umbrella has become an art form and is no

longer a part of our daily lives. If we want to enjoy the karakasa's beauty we must look to the woodblock prints of the Edo period——Harunobu shows how a karakasa in the hands of a young lady makes them both more beautiful——or to the Kabuki theater where the actor enhances the grace and flow of his dance with a karakasa. So they are there to be found if we look to the past and look to the arts. But it seems to me a shame when I stand on a busy street on a rainy day and am surrounded by acres of somber, black umbrellas relieved only occasionally by some gaudy plastic thing. I cannot help but think our sense of progress is wrong when it leads us to reject a hand-crafted object of beauty in favor of mass-produced mediocrity. I yearn for those lost days when the karakasa was in vogue.

Stephen Kohl

Sara-kobachi, 皿 小 鉢
Ceramic cups, bowls, dishes etc.,
used for table setting.

The names of China and France come readily to the mind, when one talks about richness and variety in food. These two countries are famous for the number of ingredients used to create a symphony of smells which arouse the appetite even before the food is touched.

What brings France and China closer, is also the generous use of fats and oils of all sorts. On the other hand, what separates these two countries, is the ambiance of the meal. For the Chinese, the setting and the attitude of the guests have little importance. An ordinary table, generally large and round, is soon covered with side-lipped containers, convenient for simultaneous and fast digging-in with chopsticks. In contrast, the French often request a certain decorum, including good lighting, an elegant table-cloth, and a symmetry of arrangement on the table. All these elements are part of *l'art de la table*, which presupposes a whole array of forks, knives, spoons and glasses, each one reserved for a peculiar use.

Japan differs, both from France and China, and also from other countries, in what one could call an ingrained "visual aesthetic approach." More than the taste and abundance of foods, it is their presentation which counts. For instance, fishes, vegetables, or pastes might be cut or carved in a way suggesting a flower or a fruit, or even a bird. Again, hard fried seaweed might be cut in thin strips and woven into the shape of a small basket.

Contrary to the French and the Chinese, sitting around a table, in front of each Japanese guest will be placed a small square lacquered table. On it are set several vessels (*sara-kobachi*) with different foods, in rather small quantity.

What sets the Japanese cuisine apart, is the great number and variety of shapes of these vessels. Each one may contain no more than a few beans, or slices of fish, fowl, or vegetable. Their shapes may include all sorts of bowls, deep or shallow, round or square, pentagonal or hexagonal——plus many oblong or rectangular flat plates. What makes the presentation unique in Japan, is that, besides porcelain——mostly blue and white——and earthenware with rough surfaces and subdued hues, other materials may be used, such as cut bamboo, cedar or pine plaques, and even leaves or bark.

Nowhere, in Japan, does one have an impression of overflowing abundance. The vessels are used to create a mood of infinity in a microcosm, which must be approached slowly and meditatively. Before the hand reaches for the food, the eyes must register the subtle richness of contrasts between the basic black or red lacquered table-trays and the white of the porcelain, or the reddish-brown of the earthenware.

Jean-Pierre Hauchecorne

Hanko, は ん こ
———— A stamp or seal.

The *hanko*, or personal seal, alone has legal force as a signature in Japan. Given the importance of handwriting and calligraphy in Japan, it is strange that the written signature has never achieved the place it has in the West. A seal would seem much easier to imitate than a signature, and while it is true that one can register his seal in a town or ward office, one wonders if an official can actually determine the authenticity of a seal merely by inspecting its imprint on a document.

The hanko can be a nuisance at times. Having searched one's pockets for a seal to affix on some bill only to discover that he has left it at home, one realizes with vexation the speed and simplicity of a signature. The one advantage of the hanko is that it leaves a clear and easily readable mark, whereas what passes for a signature in the West is often a shapeless, meaningless scrawl. A Japanese may have more than one seal, but many

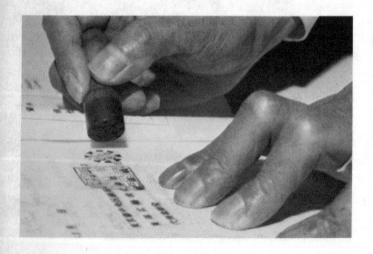

Westerners have five or six different ways of signing their names, according to mood and circumstances.

Interestingly, some of the superstitions surrounding the signature in the West have their parallels in Japan. Just as Westerners insist that they have a "lucky" signature which never fails to lead their activities to success, the Japanese use their "lucky" seal——for which they demand the finest material——on important occasions. A noble if costly material such as ivory is believed to bring luck, and the shape and style of the ideograms carved on the seal are also believed to possess varying degrees of auspiciousness. Once or twice a year some hanko maker mails me a leaflet urging that I discard my old, jagged-edged wooden seal and order a better one (the leaflet does not elaborate on how it would be better) promising that purchase of a stylish hanko would bring a marked improvement in my professional activities.

A young Japanese student I know had a seal made after obtaining his driving license. For some arcane reason, however, he did not like the look of it from the start, and complained of some nagging anxiety each time he had occasion to use it. Shortly thereafter he bought a second-hand car without even checking under the hood, and he has been plagued by continual breakdowns ever since. But he only half believes that the car dealer duped him. He still insists that there was something wrong with his hanko.

Jean-René Cholley

Soroban, そろばん
—— An abacus.

The chanting emerged from the room next door, during the silence of the lesson break. I was teaching English to businessmen at a large trading company after having been in Japan only a few weeks, and knowing little Japanese I was puzzled. It was a monotonous, almost hypnotic chant accompanied by a clicking sound like pebbles scattering on a hard surface. Thinking it to be part of a Buddhist service, I crept toward the room and peeped through the half-opened door.

Prepared for the sight of shaven heads, black robes, and burning incense, I beheld instead row upon row of young men in business suits and young ladies in company uniforms. The chanting came from a tape recorder, and I recognized numbers being called out as employees flicked the beads of their abacuses and recorded their answers. I was witnessing an arithmetic test!

Although my first encounter with the *soroban* was tinged with the esoteric, this humble-looking device can be found anywhere in Japan and comes in all sizes and colors, from tiny plastic ones in pastel shades to costly wooden models inlaid with mother-of-pearl. Every Japanese receives instruction in its use at school, and there is even a system of ranks like those in the martial arts for masters of the soroban.

Young people these days are said to prefer electronic calculators to the soroban, but it is hard to imagine that a device so intimately connected with daily life will disappear completely. Although I have heard that the highest ranking soroban master once beat a computer, I suppose this happened in the early days of computer development. Nevertheless, the soroban's portability and convenience still make it an invaluable aid in negotiations between shopkeepers. The seller will often figure the price on his soroban and show it to the buyer, who will in turn bargain by manipulating the beads, suggesting a lower price.

One's ability on the soroban, like one's ability in writing Japanese script, is based on tactile as well as visual habit. Like

the strokes which form the characters, the movements of addition, subtraction, and so on, are muscular memories stored in the fingers and arms. One commonly sees a Japanese "remembering" characters without the use of pen and paper by writing them in the air, like a conductor leading an invisible symphony orchestra. So too I recently asked a friend to add a group of numbers, and his fingers, working an invisible soroban, danced across the surface of the table. His answer was correct. Try getting any answer from an electronic calculator——*without* the calculator!

Joseph Lapenta

Furoshiki, ふろしき
—— A cloth wrapper.

I first became acquainted with the Japanese way of wrapping things when I was a student at Paris University. From time to time a Japanese scholarship student, though not officially registered, would make an appearance in the same class on classical Japanese literature that I attended, perhaps simply to kill time between lectures. Each appearance was followed by a three- or four-minute ritual in which he made himself thoroughly at home while waiting for the professor: he would invariably take the farthest seat back, put a big bundle wrapped in a dazzling green and yellow cloth on his desk, wipe his spectacles with a corner of the cloth, and proceed to unwrap the bundle. He would search the contents of his bag for some mysterious (or so it seemed to me) object, taking items out one by one and placing them on the desk or his knees, and then put everything back into place and tie the corners of the cloth——only to untie them and rummage out still more items a few moments later.

One day, my curiosity having gotten the better of me, I mustered my courage and meager Japanese to engage the student in conversation as an excuse to get a closer look at the huge bag. Accosting him at the beginning of his ritual, I managed to get a glimpse of toothbrushes, socks, a sandwich, a Japanese-French dictionary, a towel and other sundries. The sight of this hopeless jumble prompted me to ask, "Do you always carry such a cumbersome load around with you?"

The Japanese student's answer was a model of wanderlust philosophy. "My scholarship allowance is barely enough to make ends meet," he said, "but as I do not like to be tied to one place, I live out of this one *furoshiki*. When traveling, I wrap all my belongings in this cloth and take them with me. When I no longer need something, I just throw it away, and my furoshiki becomes all the lighter. At times I feel like having both hands free and I'll throw everything to the winds, fold up my cloth and put it in my pocket. This furoshiki has taught me that I really need only one-tenth of all the junk I usually carry in it. Just try to find a better suitcase than this one!"

I had to admit the logic of his argument when I returned to my seat and eyed my large attaché case, which contained only a pocket-size dictionary and ten sheets of paper.

Jean-René Cholley

Hachimaki, はちまき
A cloth tied around the head; a headband.

Headbands are a common enough sight among rugby and tennis players in the West, but nowhere do they seem to have the ceremonial or emotional significance they have in Japan. The donning of a *hachimaki* has always been associated with a "girding of the loins," a preparation for spiritual, mental or physical effort, and a strong element of combat is involved. Samurai would bind cloth around their temples before putting on their helmets, partly no doubt as padding, but also with a definite sense of resolve. Pictures of suicide pilots in the Pacific War show that this habit was deeply ingrained and retained its spiritual importance into modern times.

The wearing of the headband does not always imply warfare. Students may wear them nowadays when rioting, but they also bind their heads when preparing for examinations; neither is an otherwise soberly dressed office worker with a headband a particularly unusual sight. It is, in this instance, a symbol of the group, in a similar category as the arm band, an immediately recognizable sign that not only is there a common purpose but that one means business. Hachimaki perform a similar function at festivals and processions where the sense of group identification and preparation for physical effort are combined.

Most foreigners, however, will first encounter the headband in a sushi shop or possibly as the headgear of the traditional

Japanese carpenter and joiner. Here it is not a sense of combat or group that is intended so much as a blend of self-advertisement and self-inducement, typical of the overwhelming sense of outward show that one finds in Japan. Ever since the growth of a truly popular culture in the Tokugawa (Edo) period, a sense of panache, a sense of occasion and display, has been highly prized. Even now this panache seems to be innate in many a service worker, be he sushi delivery boy, barman, or seller of vegetables. The hachimaki acts as a reminder that it is most important to be practiced and absorbed in one's work, however humble that work may be. The ideal in Japan is, after all, not the all-round amateur but the dedicated professional.

Richard J. Bowring

Geta, 下　　駄
Japanese wooden footwear.

Originally designed to keep one's feet relatively free from dirt in muddy streets, this form of Japanese footware has a counterpart in European pattens or clogs, but the shape is quite distinctive. The flat wooden platform which forms the sole is supported by two thin lateral slats so arranged as to allow the platform to tip forward easily, and the whole is attached by means of a thong which passes between the first and second toe and then divides over the top of the foot. This is common to most other types of Japanese footwear such as zori and *waraji*. A somewhat unusual feature of this kind of arrangement is that the thong is fixed along the centre line, not towards the inner side where it would conform with the shape of the foot. As a result, if the wearer wishes to keep both feet straight the geta will point inwards; conversely, if the geta are straight the feet will be pointing outwards. But this does not cause any noticeable inconvenience and there has been little attempt to change this as far as traditional geta are concerned.

It is in the rainy season and the damp heat of the summer that geta come into their own, for the wood is cooler than leather and infinitely preferable to plastic. Compared with clogs, the surface area in contact with the ground is reduced to a minimum and so less mud is collected around the sole in bad conditions. They are also possibly the best prevention against athelete's foot, which a glance at advertisements in Japan during the summer will quickly reveal is a highly prevalent complaint.

Although essentially part of Japanese dress, geta are by no means out of place with trousers or jeans, but this combination has a very informal, relaxed air about it. Partly because of the damage they might cause to modern flooring and partly because they are very definitely outdoor wear, they are inconvenient and are only really used for neighbourhood walks. There is also the question of their noise value, however, which, while not too desirable in a public library, is undoubtedly an added attraction.

The *kara-koro* sound of geta, like the noise of wooden clappers as the fire watchman makes his rounds on dry winter nights, is all part of the equipment of nostalgia that one guards with zealous care.

Richard J. Bowring

Mimikaki, 耳かき

An instrument used for cleaning
wax from the ears.

Where else but in Japan, and hopefully still in China, could one expect to find sentimentality and romance associated with such a mundane hygienic instrument as the ear pick?

I recall with no great pleasure the sanitary ordeals of my thoroughly Western upbringing in Japan. Along with the mandatory purges so irritating to a young boy——brushing teeth, cleaning fingernails, scrubbing the back of the neck, and even the weekly bath——a periodic removal of wax from the ear was compulsory.

As far as I was concerned, this was strictly a repulsive, clinical process involving medicated swabs. Little did I know then that all around me were millions of Japanese girls and boys who enjoyed and appreciated this attention from their mothers, or that for the adult Japanese male this intimate ritual, when performed by his wife or lover, was not only a sensual gratification but also, in a very Japanese sense, a service symbolic of the utmost mutual trust and affection.

To understand the warm memories of childhood and the pleasant sensations the lowly ear pick conjures up in the Japanese mind, it is necessary to recall that the Japanese have traditionally lived without furniture, sleeping and sitting on floors covered with rush matting. Thus, the nostalgic image most commonly associated by Japanese with the ear pick is one of relaxed, secure comfort in the home——of a child lying with his head in his mother's lap.

For Japanese steeped in romantic literature, however, the image evoked may be of a happy marriage relationship or of a man and his mistress, since this labor of love has been celebrated for centuries in Japanese novels and poetry.

Partisans of "Women's Lib" should note that in adult Japanese society it is only the men who are so accommodated and never the other way around. But for the man who wishes to enjoy such attention, who must lie prone and vulnerable to the possibility of accidental or willful injury, his self-surrender symbolizes absolute security and confidence in his partner. And for the traditionally minded Japanese woman, the mere demonstration of such trust is sufficient to inspire gratitude and tender sentiments.

As might be imagined, the instrument itself may be found in various degrees of refinement and value. The cheapest and most common type of ear pick is a simple bamboo implement rounded out and curved slightly at the tip. The materials for others range from metallic to beautifully carved, delicate ivory. I was not even surprised a short time ago when I received, along with perhaps five hundred other guests attending the inaugural ceremonies at a new, ultramodern chemical plant, an ear pick plated with 18-karat gold and emblazoned with the company's trademark as the souvenir of the occasion one inevitably receives at such receptions in Japan.

Walter Nichols

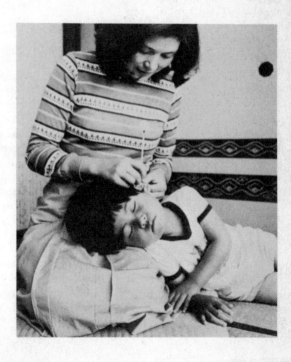

Meoto-jawan, 夫婦茶碗
Matched rice bowls with connotations of "his" and "hers."

Meoto-jawan are matching rice bowls used by husband and wife while dining alone, with family and friends, or on other occasions which are not strictly formal. Similarly, *meoto yunomi-jawan* are tea cups for married couples used in the same fashion. Related to this concept of matching articles for husband and wife are *meoto-bashi*, two pairs of chopsticks, and also a special set of two futon, large mattress-like cushions for sleeping, which like other paired household items may be brought by the bride when she marries.

When interviewed regarding their knowledge and feeling about meoto-jawan and other paired objects, almost without exception individuals stated that these articles dated from *mukashi*, long ago, and stressed and frequently valued what they conceived to be their traditional nature. Indeed these objects are traditional as they represent continuities through time, but the short span of that continuity is surprising. Apparently meoto-jawan (and presumably some other paired items) first were used by the merchant class at the end of the Edo period, became popular fashion during the Meiji period and were even more commonly used in the Taishô period (1912-1926). It is said by some that originally meoto-jawan were the same size but that during the Meiji period the husband's *chawan* was made larger than the wife's, owing perhaps to the social climate of the times.

To many the most obvious feature of meoto-jawan and other paired items is the difference in size, possibly leading contemporary liberation-minded commentators to perceive in this the inequality of the sexes in Japanese society. That these household objects do reflect certain aspects of Japanese life is undeniable; but that these necessarily and predominantly represent inequality between husband and wife does not obtain in all cases since many egalitarian young people yet use these paired objects although there appears to be a trend towards equalization of size.

I feel that more useful a perspective than relative size is that of sustenance. Meoto-jawan, meoto yunomi-jawan, meoto-bashi and paired futon are all associated with food, drink, sleep and procreation. Recalling the words of Elizabeth Barrett Browning in her *Sonnets from the Portuguese*, on this "level of everyday's most quiet need," I find a concrete symbolization of the intimate and vital interdependency of man and woman. In daily use these paired household items may serve as tangible reminders of the most basic pan-human reality of survival.

Anne Elizabeth Murase

Hashi, 著
Chopsticks.

There can be few things so immediately evocative of Far Eastern culture as a pair of chopsticks. Only to be found in the major areas of Chinese influence, these simple, hygienic implements are eminently suitable for the kind of food which has made Oriental cooking famous. Depending on one's taste they conjure up the clean, smooth texture of sashimi or the more robust delights of Chinese cuisine. The delicate flavour of the former is in no danger of being spoiled by that metallic taste which knives and forks might well impart, and for cooking and eating oily dishes they are the most practical and efficient drainer imaginable.

There is, of course, a major difference between the Chinese and Japanese varieties. Chinese chopsticks are invariably longer, thicker and made of ivory (or now, unfortunately, plastic); this makes them unusually difficult to wield without practice and many is the foreigner who must have been agreeably surprised when arriving in Japan to find the smaller, wooden chopsticks so much easier to use. No more of that surreptitious stabbing of meat balls.

The chief contribution of Japanese culture is undoubtedly the transformation of chopsticks from mere implements to objects of aesthetic pleasure, a natural outcome of the fact that in the Japanese cuisine the aesthetic appeal is one of the elements. Rules governing the correct use of chopsticks abound, but the foreigner need only use his common sense and refrain from picking up objects from the floor with his *hashi* or, in extremely polite circles, from serving himself from a central dish with his own pair.

Chopsticks have also had their role in ceremony, and in particular are associated with Buddhist cremations. As a result, there are a few major taboos concerning their use which it might be as well to remember. Never pass food from one to another by means of one's own chopsticks, for this brings to mind the

ceremony of passing the bones of the deceased by members of the family. Secondly, never stick your chopsticks vertically into the rice. This too connotes death; a bowl of rice with chopsticks standing upright is offered to the dead in the family shrine. Thirdly, when on a picnic make sure to break your chopsticks in two after use, lest a wily devil find them and use them for his own nefarious ends.

Richard J. Bowring

Fugu, ふ.   ぐ
Blowfish; prized as a delicacy.

For *fugu* the dictionary gives: "a swellfish; a globefish; a puffer." As for compounds, there are "swellfish poisoning" and "swellfish soup." Neither of these will do, really, because, as will be seen, "swellfish poisoning" has delicate ritual elements which demand something more elegant and mysterious, and "swellfish soup" sounds most nauseous, when the dish to which it refers is delicious. One is almost tempted to render literally the characters with which fugu is written, "river-pig." This has a certain whimsical charm, except for the fact that the fugu is a salt-water fish, and why it is called a river-pig no one seems to know. So the word must be numbered among the untranslatables. That is unfortunate, because the fugu is the sacred object of the sort of cult the Japanese like best.

It is eminently edible, but only for a few months each year, which fact gives it the sense of remoteness and elusiveness one asks of sacred objects. There are restaurants which are open only for the three or four good fugu months. The rest of the year they stand grandly silent, like fallen castles or deserted cathedrals.

The meat of the fugu is very good to eat, but it really looks better than it tastes, and so is an admirable object of culinary mysteries. It has a pearly-white color and can be sliced paper thin, and it can be fabricated into the most marvelous arabesques and rosettes. One looks at them as at a work of art and is loathe to disturb them, and when finally one has a bite, it has in it the delicious taste of blasphemy, as of eating an altarpiece.

But the most important fact is that parts of the fugu are poisonous. Some months ago a famous Kabuki actor died of eating fugu, and the newspapers carried the names of well-known people who had come to the same end in the past. There was a certain reverend quality to the lists, as of lists of holy martyrs.

The other day there was another fugu story in the papers: a number of proprietors of fugu restaurants gathered on the banks of the Sumida River and threw some fugu in, by way of praying, it was said, that swellfish poisoning claim no more victims. One suspects that the real motives were different, to keep people in mind of the danger. A cult worthy of the name should have its dangers and claim its victims from time to time.

Edward G. Seidensticker

Matsutake, まつたけ

A kind of mushroom (*Armillaria edodes*).

Fairly large as edible mushrooms go, the *matsutake* is beige and brown on the outside and has firm, white flesh. Although it is often considered an exclusively Japanese mushroom, it is found in Taiwan, Korea, China, and parts of the United States. It grows in groves of coniferous trees, especially the red pine—hence the name *matsu* (pine) *take* (mushroom)—in several parts of the main Japanese island, Honshû. But matsutake from a certain part of the ancient capital city, Kyoto, are considered the most delicious and fragrant.

The taste of the matsutake is pleasant, but it is the odor that captures the Japanese fancy. It is a delicate, woody fragrance that is impossible to describe or forget. The matsutake is served in a variety of more or less elaborate dishes, but the best way to capture its full aroma and to enjoy its flavors is to shred it lengthwise, toast it lightly over an open fire, and eat it with a small amount of salt or soy sauce. The popular seasonal delicacy called *dobin-mushi* is another excellent dish revealing the matsutake to good advantage. This favorite food is a lightly flavored broth with white fish, chicken, a distinctively flavored plant called *mitsuba* (trefoil), and small matsutake. Dobin-mushi is served in attractive individual pottery containers.

Because it is harvested only once a year, in the autumn, the matsutake, though cultivated, remains expensive. The price may be somewhat lower in the regions where it is grown; but in the greengrocers and department stores of Tokyo, at the opening of the season, matsutake sometimes sell for as much as fifteen or twenty dollars a pound. Even at these high prices, however, the Japanese consider the mushroom such a treat that the dealers rarely find it necessary to cut rates to clear their shelves of the commodity.

In addition to its flavor and aroma, the matsutake has a shape that has long endeared it to the people of Japan. To their way of looking at things, it is decidedly phallic. For this reason, it is used in conjunction with the clam, the traditional symbol for the female genitalia, in designs for ceramic sake cups sold in souvenir shops near the famous Great Ise Shrine. Drinking from these cups ostensibly ensures fertility. In comic scroll pictures, the phallic matsutake, dressed as a Buddhist priest, appears in ribald situations to satirize licentious behavior. It is as a result of associations of this kind that each autumn diminutive, kimono-clad ladies are often seen giggling demurely behind their fans as they pass the counters where matsutake mushrooms are sold.

Richard L. Gage

Hatsugatsuo, 初 が つ お
——The first bonito of the season.

> *Me ni wa aoba*   Behold the green leaves!
> *Yamahototogisu*   A thrush singing in the hills——
> *Hatsugatsuo*   The first bonito
>   —Sodô (1642–1716)

It is the first month of summer in the lunar calendar——May in our Gregorian——and the verdant hills are alive with song. Sodô sits down at a country inn to a meal of sliced raw bonito served on freshly cut bamboo leaves. Eating the first bonito of the season, the haiku poet partakes in the ageless Japanese rite of celebrating man's closeness to the cycle of nature.

The Japanese have an appreciation for the change of season which approaches reverence, and they savor each season with every one of their senses, including their palates. Restaurant menus boast of seasonal cuisine the year round, and the bonito, prized for its rich flavor, is a favorite even among seasonal dishes. In May the bonito migrate to the seas near Japan as faithfully as the deciduous forests sprout new leaves. The Japanese eat the fish raw (why spoil the taste by cooking it?) and although they claim that early bonito are not as delicious as those in high season, they value the first even more perhaps than the best.

This sort of reverence is hard for us to understand. Not only have we in the West divorced our lives long ago from the seasons, our standards of freshness compare pitiably to those of the Japanese. We do not talk of the "first Hereford," the "first wheat," or the "first coffee," but Japanese speak joyously of the first rice, tea, or this or that fish——the very staples of the Japanese diet——to appear in season. And we may like our meat and vegetables fresh, but not enough to go shopping every day for them, as do the Japanese. Multiple crops, canned foods, and freezers have dulled our taste buds, and convenience has had the last word.

Sadly, Japan's zeal to industrialize has profaned that special reverence for nature's cycle. The land and waters have been sacrificed to support a huge urban population settled amid forests of utility poles, seas of asphalt, and hills of garbage. Each year fishermen sail further out from shore to ensure a pollution-free catch. The time may come when bonito no longer frequent Japanese waters in May. Fearful that Sodô's centuries-old verse has lost its significance in the seasonless, urban setting, I contribute, with regret, another:

Me ni wa haiki	Behold the smog!
Dotto kuiuchi	A pounding pile driver——
Osengome	Contaminated rice
	Guy Jean

Satsumaimo, さつまいも
—— The sweet potato.

The sweet potato is like literature itself, and so perhaps it is just as well that there are no poets who write about sweet potatoes (leastways I cannot at the moment think of any). Poems about poetry tend to be rather unsatisfactory affairs, self-conscious and precious. A poem about a sweet potato probably would be too.

Most great literature is an immediately recognizable fact. Almost anyone can see it for what it is, and be affected. And on the other hand it is an entity of infinite complexity, into which the lives of a millennium of scholars and critics can go, and the work still not be at an end.

So it is with the sweet potato. Where did it come from, and how did it get to all the places where it is? No one really knows. Its path can be traced from America to Europe and

thence to the Middle East and parts of the Orient. But how did it get to places like Hawaii, where it was undoubtedly present before Columbus discovered America? Did it perhaps not originate in America at all? Or were there pre-Columbian migrations westwards from America? These are the problems upon which the scholars labor, and the answer to most of them would seem to be that there is no final answer, and probably never will be. Is not the sweet potato then a better symbol for literature than say the plum or the wistaria, which do not raise any very considerable or pause-giving problems?

What the sweet potato is as a fact, on the other hand, is immediately apparent, and very important: it is life itself for straitened and marginal populations. We are told that its effect, when it came to Japan in the seventeenth century and spread throughout the land in the eighteenth century, was to open inhospitable expanses to habitation and introduce a new kind of poverty——to make life precariously possible for people who without it would have died young or not been born. People came to live on certain barren but beautiful islands, a new class of marginal labor was produced for exploiters to exploit, and so everyone was a little better off.

The sweet potato has continued to be a symbol of the struggle to survive. Those of us who saw Japan in the years after the surrender and before the Korean War saw a land of sweet-potato eaters. It was a land of brave people refusing to give up, and the sweet potato was the chief thing that kept them going. And have they improved in every way in the years since? Perhaps it is not just sentimental nostalgia which makes some of us think that the struggling Japanese of those days was in some respects superior to the affluent Japanese of today.

Edward G. Seidensticker

Nigirimeshi, にぎりめし
A rice-ball (alt. *o-nigiri; o-musubi*).

I had heard of *nigirimeshi* before I had enjoyed their particular flavor, but I had not known that they could actually be categorized as delicious. My earliest recollection of eating nigirimeshi goes back to one very warm June day in Hiroshima. At that time I was teaching at a boys' school, and on the first semester outing we huffed and puffed up a small mountain on the western edge of the city. It was one of my first times to be with the boys in more relaxed surroundings.

With much shouting and laughing we drank from our water bottles and started in on our lunches. I had the usual American delicacies——ham and cheese and peanut butter and jam——and was enjoying myself after the hot climb when one of the boys said, "Sensei, how about trying one of these? My mother made them." The student peered out expectantly from under the brim of his hat, obviously feeling sorry for someone who had to get by with just ordinary sandwiches. I had a pretty good idea what it was, but I played dumb——often a very wise course in Japan ——and asked him what that glob of rice wrapped in some sort of leaf was. I had guessed correctly: it was indeed nigirimeshi, but he assured me that it was a tasty treat.

I have been eating nigirimeshi ever since for the past ten or so years, and while I admit they are not my favorite Japanese food, still they have possibilities which the English-language description——a handful of rice wrapped with seaweed and containing a bit of salted fish, or fish eggs, or maybe a salted plum——just does not convey to the Western ear. *Meshi* means cooked rice and *nigiri* means gripping or squeezing. Rice has been an important molder of Japanese tastes, being the staple food in Japan for the last two thousand years. Made simply by shaping the rice with one's salt-smeared palms into triangular balls, nigirimeshi is, to any Japanese who is very hungry or pressed for time, an incomparably delicious meal——the very staff of life, if you will.

I do not exaggerate. Not long ago I read a front-page story in the newspaper about a hijacked airplane whose mostly Japanese passengers were held at gunpoint for several days. When the airplane finally landed at Athens International Airport, a contingent of local Japanese awaited them with a boxload of—you've guessed it—nigirimeshi.

Charles Hancock

Sushi, す　し
Sliced, usually raw seafood
over rice-balls.

The first time is the most difficult. Thoughts of slimy, malodorous, blood-red pieces of raw fish in my mouth had effectively blunted any desire to wander into a sushi shop. Whenever my Japanese friends asked what I thought about this unique cuisine, I answered that except for fruits and vegetables I preferred my food cooked. But after hearing so many Japanese and foreigners rave about sushi, I decided it was time to stand up to the challenge. A nearby sushi shop served as the testing ground. My first reaction was: it's delicious! And I kept asking myself why I had waited so long to enjoy this gourmet's treat.

What then is sushi? Basically, it's a slice of fish on a small mound of rice with a dab of Japanese horseradish (*wasabi*) in between. While this recipe may sound relatively simple, every aspect of making sushi requires special knowledge. Only the highest quality rice is used and it is cooked and seasoned with vinegar, salt, and sugar in a manner that is almost impossible to duplicate in one's kitchen. The fish, of course, is the most important part of sushi. Contrary to my original notion, the fish in sushi shops never exudes an unpleasant odor because only the freshest fish is used. Moreover, only the choicest sections of the fish end up in front of the customer. This means that a large portion of the fish is discarded; and sometimes, in the case of smaller fish, the man behind the counter gets just one serving from the fish.

Picking up the mouth-size piece of sushi with either your hand or with chopsticks, you should dip it in the small saucer of soy sauce and then insert the whole piece into your mouth. If you try to bite it into smaller pieces, you will probably discover that raw fish does not give so easily. Along with the sushi you eat slices of fresh pickled ginger and drink Japanese tea, beer, or sake. There are several kinds and styles of sushi. Many different fish are used in sushi shops, but the most popular seem to be tuna, cuttlefish, octopus, eel, shrimp, mackerel, and shellfish.

Since I was only familiar with such "exotic" fish as trout and bass before coming to Japan, it was a pleasant surprise to experience the wide variety of fish enjoyed by the Japanese. Along with raw fish, there are sushi made with egg omelets, seaweed, and certain vegetables. Not all the fish is raw, by the way; some is boiled, some cooked, and some marinated.

The Japanese eat more fish than do practically any other people on earth, and of all the ways to prepare fish, sushi is one of their most favorite. For those people with a sense of culinary adventure and a desire to enjoy Japanese culture, a visit to a sushi shop is a must. But beware: addiction to sushi can be very expensive. And it is a habit extremely hard to break.

Thomas J. Cogan

Instanto Râmen, インスタント・ラーメン
—"Instant *râmen*"; a precooked, dehydrated
noodle dish.

It is not rice that the Japanese have a voracious appetite for.
It is noodles. While Western foods have made conspicuous
inroads in their eating habits, traditional noodle slurping has just
as conspicuously increased in popularity. These parallel trends
may in fact be connected. Western-style dishes are appreciated
for their advantage of quick convenience, compared with the
time that goes into preparing and eating a regular Japanese meal.
And it was to exploit the demand for such that *insutanto
râmen*, the first instant food product using a Japanese recipe,
was invented. That was in 1958, and Japan has not been the
same since. More than the hamburger is in America, the quickly
made bowl of noodles is the most ubiquitous artifact in modern
Japan.

Of course, the Japanese have been consuming noodles for
centuries, and probably for the same prime reason they do
today. A bowl of noodles was always a fast snack, which would
have a certain attraction in any era. The contemplative life——to
draw an extreme contrast with today's life-style——would be
congenial to a meal of minimal fuss and bother. It remained,
however, for mid-20th century science to prove how minimal
you can get.

Of the variety of standard noodle recipes, râmen, or so-called
Chinese noodles, was chosen for instantizing. This consists of
long, thin pasta and a soy sauce flavored broth, to which a few
thin slices of pork and a bit of vegetables are added. The nour-
ishment is not great but the steaming hot bowl, attacked with a
gusto permitted only for it, is irresistible. In the convenient,
packaged form it is the cheapest meal that can be had. Since the
first insutanto râmen product came onto the market, many
refinements have appeared. Everything but the bowl may be
included in the package. Even that has been provided with the
latest version, called "Cup Noodles." This comes in a paper cup,
to which you only have to add hot water. Now there are vend-

ing machines that provide the hot water, too.

A few statistics from the Japan Convenience Food Industry Association give breadth to the subject. In 1974, the Japanese consumed 3,770,000,000 bowls of insutanto râmen. And in the same year ¥2,180,000,000 worth of the stuff was exported to 60 countries, while more was manufactured under licenses in six countries. For depth on the subject, it seems appropriate to use a quick contemplative cliche of our day: the implications are mind-boggling.

Holloway Brown

Fûrin, 風　　鈴
A hanging bell that tinkles in
the wind.

Summer. The thick heat moves in to occupy and oppress the
city. Echoing the seasonal Kabuki fare, nighttime TV programs
are filled with horror films designed to induce shivers against the
heat, while the rhythmic clack of the geta of those taking a
cooling evening walk echo into the late night. Eel teriyaki is
hawked as the "stamina food" to put some zip into spirits
drooping from suffocating subways and steam-radiator streets. In
the old part of town where neighbors are often friends of
generations and apartment houses have not altogether replaced
Japanese wood-frame houses, doors may be flung open of an
evening and old men sit in their underwear on the verandas,
talking, playing go, fanning themselves with round fans. And
through it all, the heat and the heaviness, from the window
ledges of sixth floor apartments as well as the eaves of steep-
sloping tile roofs, comes the clear, cool, other-worldly echo of
the small *fûrin*.

The Japanese seem to enjoy defining their seasons by the
foods they eat and certain very special images and sounds. These
may, as in the case of the February plum blossoms (proclaiming
the advent of spring in defiance of snowbound trains, skier-
clogged mountains and chilblains earned in one's own home),
seem to a Westerner to contradict the very time of year they are
meant to evoke. It is almost as though the reality can be manipulated by concentration on a particular symbol, like a kind of
mandala.

Just how inviolable the assignation of these seasonal symbols
may be was demonstrated to me recently when I let slip to
some Japanese friends that I kept my fûrin out in winter as well
as in summer. Their mock horror dissolved into uncontrolled
laughter as I defensively revealed that my reason was to coax
some reminiscences of summer warmth into my more-than-chilly
Japanese house.

However, symbolism aside, I have always loved the wind bell,

ever since its charming tinkle brought me the first consolation in the record heat wave that was my initiation into Tokyo summers. Quite lovely and delicate in shape, it nevertheless costs very little, even though made of metal; therefore it is accessible to all, a small pleasurable object in everyone's daily life.

And yet, once the metal is awakened to its natural vibrations, the enchanted echo never seems to disappear. The clear, magical reverberations hold out the tantalizing promise of one day carrying the listener gently off and away from the murky discomforts of this world to wherever the sound travels.

Sharon Ann Rhoads

Tatami, た た み
Rush-covered mats used for
flooring.

Tatami is the soft creak and caress of a field of grass at your feet and the sweet smell of straw in the morning. It is like carpeting your living room with an early autumn evening.

The tatami is a straw mat covered with a fine layer of woven rush. It is about two and a half to three inches thick and the size and shape of a single bed——three feet wide and six feet long. The size is not coincidental, for the tatami originally served as a bed or mattress placed on a raised platform as was the custom in Europe.

The general use of tatami does not date back as far as one might think. It was only four or five hundred years ago that it became the mainstay of Japanese interior decorating. Formerly there were only one or two mats in a room, but with time the Japanese found them so comfortable and convenient that they were eventually to cover the floor of nearly the entire house. Replacing or superseding most kinds of furniture used in the West, the tatami is more, not less modern than the traditional Occidental beds, tables, and chairs.

There is an old saying in Japan: "The tatami, like a wife, is best when new," and like some wives, the tatami, once it moved in, gradually took over the whole house and became a major influence on the mode of living in Japan. The Japanese adjusted their lives to the clean, soft tatami and began to live and work closer to the floor. Even the arts of Japan——tea ceremony, flower arrangement, dance, and music——have adjusted to the leisurely tempo dictated by life on the tatami and have been refined in the process.

Tatami are responsible for much of the distinctive qualities of a Japanese house. Open, airy houses with raised floors keep the tatami away from the damp ground. Bedding is folded up and put away in closets during the day so as not to clutter the room; and because there is little other heavy furniture which cuts into the matting, even small houses give a feeling of spaciousness. Shoes are left just inside the main entrance to save the tatami from wear and tear and dirt. There are few carpets as soft and as comfortable as the fresh-smelling tatami.

John Herrick

Shoji, 障　子
Latticed, paper-covered window
or sliding door.

I had known of the quiet dignity of traditional Japanese
houses but had seldom experienced the actual delight until my
first visit to a potter's in the outskirts of Kyoto on an annoy-
ingly muggy summer afternoon. I was kept waiting in a spacious
tatami room for so long that the sun began setting, filtering
through the translucent shoji-paper. The afterglow slowly
changed the still hay-color of the tatami floor into fleeting
shades of vermilion. Simultaneously, the shoji-paper's creamy
color turned into subdued ochres, creating a soft, dusky atmosphere, then near darkness. With night approaching, I turned on a
light that made shoji look surprisingly white. Onto the paper,
every line of neat latticework cast a black shadow which grew
progressively thicker in proportion to its distance from the light.
The dark lines of the lattice and its shadow, woven onto the
shoji screen, looked like a Japanese rendition of black-and-white
Mondrian. Moving closer, my fuzzy, giant silhouette became a
shadow play with the shoji as the stage.

I was not the only star, however. Another step nearer and my
eyes met another's, peering from behind the shoji. A moment
later they vanished, leaving only a hole, obviously freshly poked.
I slid back the shoji and saw the mischievous boy running away,
undoubtedly curious about the foreign guest. He must have had
such fun on other occasions, for I noticed that small rectangles
of new paper had replaced his previous peepholes.

That brief invasion of privacy stirred new thoughts of what
shoji was all about. Certainly its fragile paper invites poking
fingers and listening ears, and requires repair; its wooden frame
lacks a surface for knocking and keyholes for locking. The
sliding panels serve as doors, windows, a means of admitting
light, and as light-weight enclosures easily removed to combine
with adjacent space. Unlike the solid Western door and wall that
protect man from the elements, shoji was meant to mediate
between man and nature, thus fulfilling a harmonious relation-

ship basic to the native life-style. The frame, rattled by winds, and the paper, darkened by age, enhance the delicate balance between aesthetics and function, and enrich the sensations of nature. Rain, snow, wind and clouds transform the impressions of shoji as seasons come and go.

Bringing me back to the original purpose of my visit, the master himself slid open the shoji. Silently I thanked him for such a memorable introduction.

Sally Lynne McCreary

Tokobashira, 床　柱

An alcove post, used in decorating the *tokonoma*.

In the most important rooms of the traditional Japanese house is usually an alcove for the display of a few selected ornaments. The alcove is called the *tokonoma*, and the non-structural post forming the boundary between it and whatever is beside it——ornamental shelves, cupboard, empty space——is called the *tokobashira*. Under ordinary circumstances the post is square in section with beveled corners. But variations are possible. For example, round posts are sometimes used for a rustic effect. In the highly refined, sometimes finicky and precious, style of the teahouse, natural tree trunks complete with bark and twists and bends are used as tokobashira. The tokonoma in the stately mansions of the wealthy during past ages were vast affairs demanding appurtenances of corresponding size and

grandeur. The tokobashira in these alcoves were usually decorated with gilded and elaborately tooled bronze peg covers called *kugikakushi*.

In modern Japanese traditional architecture the tokobashira has preserved its importance as a kind of spatial status symbol. So vital is it thought to be that sometimes architects deliberately omit it from a tokonoma to create a startling effect. If talented contemporary architects put this old design element to good effect, men of lesser abilities not infrequently abuse it. Tokonoma and tokobashira are always found in the Japanese-style rooms of hotels. But nowadays, in place of an elegant scroll painting or a vase of tastefully arranged flowers, the tokonoma in these establishments enshrines the television set. In harmony with this mood the tokobashira is generally of brightly varnished, knotty, bumpy wood probably purchased for imagined aesthetic appeal but used in a way that suggests nothing so much as brown toad skin.

The Japanese mind thrives on ambivalence. Things are not what they seem, yet they are not *not* what they seem. The word tokobashira and its parts illuminate this paradox. The *hashira* (bashira for euphony) part is straightforward enough: it means "post." The *toko* part means bed; but in Japanese usage it also means the tatami-covered floor. To further elaborate the situation, the Japanese use the word toko, written with the same character, to mean the bedding spread on the floor. A person with a penchant for semantic exactitude would be puzzled to know whether he should think of the tokobashira as a floorpost or a bedpost. In typical Japanese fashion, it is neither and both, because the floor is both the floor and the bed. The *Daikanwa Jiten*, a many-volume dictionary of Chinese characters used in the Japanese language, seems to favor the bedpost interpretation since it gives as an example of usage of the word tokobashira a quotation from a work by Ihara Saikaku, an author noted for his eroticism.

Richard L. Gage

Futon, ふ と ん

Bedding; bedclothes; quilt;
coverlet.

The futon is the place for sleep, but is not in the least like a
bed because, for one thing, it is movable and, for another, it is
on the floor. A bed is a heavy, static thing. It is a wooden box
on legs and has a great deal in common with a coffin. A bed
demands a special room be dedicated to the sacred mysteries of
birth, death and copulation which are celebrated in its depths.
The futon sleeps one flat on the ground, and is not an item of
furniture. It is a movable collection of bedding. So it allows the
ultimate functions of life to take place within everyday living
space and sleeping, sickness, making love are activities without
apartness.

They take place in the area which is also used for eating,
working and performing all the secular business of life. If one's
futon were suitably arranged, it would be entirely possible, for
example, to give birth to a baby in comfort whilst keeping an
eye on the soup. Many Japanese women must have done so. The
futon means the rooms in a Japanese house are not restricted in
function. Any room can become a bedroom; any number of
people can sleep in any room. Sleeping space becomes living
space and living space sleeping space at will, or need. In the
overcrowding of the great cities, foldaway bedding means that
one-room living is a more discreet and seemly affair.

At bedtime in Japan, we slide open the door of the fitted
cupboard——a feature of every home, even the most modest——
and from it we take out the bedding we have neatly stored there
during the day. It is equally easy to get out of bed: you just roll
from the covers onto the tatami.

A family can sleep just as many visitors as it has futon; there
is no such thing as a spare bed in Japan, only a question of
sufficient floor. I once stayed with a family of nine sisters in a
room the tatami of which was seamlessly tiled with futon; there
was no floor left on which there was not a sleeper. In Japan,
sleeping, however chaste, is a private activity only for those who

live by themselves. We all went to sleep and woke up in unison; I wonder what insomniacs in large families do. Half an hour later, the futon were hanging from the balcony to air, like so many banners.

The futon must be put out to air in the open every day or it will become damp and unhealthy; it will also become damp and unhealthy if it is left on the floor all day. So hygiene as well as convenience dictates that the household futons should be, first, aired in the sun, and, second, put away and *not* used as a sprawling place by the lazy when not in use as bedding. This is part of the ecology of social arrangements; tamper with one part of it——substitute an immovable bed for futon in a four and a half mat room——and the whole fragile structure loses its logic.

Angela Carter

Kotatsu, こ た つ
A warmer or heating element,
with frame and coverlet.

At Kôya-san in 1941 I first encountered the *kotatsu*. It was a late autumn day, cold and windy, and my friends and I arrived, chilled to the bone, at the temple where we were to stay. No sooner had I put my feet inside the waiting kotatsu than I thought: What a wonderful invention this is! It was only after another thirty minutes or so that I began to experience one of the disadvantages of the kotatsu: my feet were as warm as toast, but at the same time, in that otherwise unheated room, the upper part of my body was all but blue with cold.

Since that day so many years ago I've often wondered about the Japanese reaction to temperature, in many ways so contradictory as to be a real puzzle to the Western observer. For example, the kotatsu itself represents a real concern with keeping the feet warm, an ingenious solution to a problem that faces much of the world. And yet the same student who hugs so closely to its warmth will suddenly go outside, even in the snow, wearing only geta, and for hours on end show no sign of discomfort.

Another example, in reverse, is the way Japanese stop swimming in late August: no matter how hot the weather in September, the average Japanese would never think of cooling off in the sea. And then there are the woolen *haramaki*, worn even on the hottest summer day.

All of which suggests to me that human reactions to heat and cold are as much a matter of social custom as of physiology. Doubtless some of our Western customs in this regard must appear equally strange to the traditionally oriented Japanese (if there are any of that breed left). Having said all of which, I must confess that I myself have a *hori-gotatsu* (sunken kotatsu) in my Tokyo home. I use it with the greatest of pleasure the year round, putting an electric warmer in it for winter and, in summer, opening small doors in the sides to let in the cool air from under the house. So I still think it a wonderful invention.

But I do draw the line at the haramaki, just as I enjoy swimming as late as October or even November. In a way, I suppose, I'm fortunate in being able to enjoy the best of both worlds, East and West.

Meredith Weatherby

Engawa, えんがわ
—— Veranda-like porch.

One of my neighbors lives modestly but comfortably in completely traditional Japanese style. His house, built more than a century ago, opens onto a formal Japanese garden which makes his home a sanctuary from the surrounding confusion of modern Japan.

Though I have occasionally been invited to visit with Mr. Sekiguchi, I have never actually been inside his house. That is to say, we always sit and talk on his *engawa*, or Japanese-style porch, to which I am invariably ushered from the gate via the garden.

Volumes have been written about the beautiful simplicity of Japanese residential architecture and much about its adaptability, by means of sliding panels, to the Japanese love of communion with Nature. But usually overlooked are the problems of heating and privacy in a home with virtually no solid walls. And it is the engawa which serves these structural and social needs.

Physically, this especially unique feature of Japanese architecture is more like a loggia than a veranda. Though actually an integral, enclosable part of the house, it is functionally a neutral space between outdoors and indoors. In fine weather it can be opened completely to attract cool breezes or to provide an unobstructed view of the garden. Completely closed off in cold or inclement weather, it serves as insulation or protection from the elements. From the interior it may be viewed as an extension of floor space. From the outside, since there are no railings and it is only a stone-step up from the ground, the engawa may be viewed as an adjunct of the garden.

Socially, the engawa serves many purposes. This is where the children play. It is here that the old folks can bask in the sun while working at odd chores. And it is here that casual visitors can be offered hospitality without violating the privacy of the home——neighbors like myself, perhaps, a policeman on his

rounds, or the weary postman. Japanese etiquette requires the extension of courtesies——at least a cup of tea——to any caller. But if invited into the house, a visitor must be received with great formality. The engawa provides the perfect middle ground between these extremes.

Sadly, all my other neighbors have abandoned their Japanese life-style for cramped apartments with elevators, steam heat and air conditioning. They live sealed off from Nature and must either dispose of visitors at the door or invite them inside. And surely they must look down at Mr. Sekiguchi sunning himself on his engawa, in his house yet also in his garden, with envy and nostalgia.

Walter Nichols

Sentô, 錢　湯
Public bath, bathhouse (alt.
furoya).

Most Japanese homes have baths nowadays, but the *sentô* still fulfills a public need in the cities and there is one located within walking distance of virtually wherever you might reside. For students and other single persons living in rooms and cheap apartments, the clean, inexpensive sentô is a necessity of daily living in Japan.

My Japanese "father" (that is, my host and guardian) took me to a sentô the very first evening I spent in Japan, and as I stepped up to the area where the men change their clothes I thought I had walked into a nudist camp. I became terribly self-conscious, never before having stripped in public, and although I hid my embarrassment and began casually washing myself, I never did regain my composure. After about ten minutes I left, although "Father" was still in the middle of washing his hair.

Today, two years later, the sentô is one of the pleasures of life for me and I frequent it regularly, clip-clopping in my geta, with wash bowl under my arm. In those first days in Japan I was repulsed by the thought of a dozen or so people all soaking at once in one big tub, but now I feel completely at ease and go about bathing in a manner far more thorough than I ever did at home in Hong Kong. Humming a tune to myself as I scrub, soak, scrub and soak again, I emerge from the bath with both body and spirit cleansed, my day-to-day troubles and fatigue seemingly rinsed away with the grime.

For insights into society the sentô is ideal. One commonly sees young girls in the men's bathing section. The Japanese do not consider this mixed bathing, however, because, after all, little girls are just little girls they say——a reflection, perhaps, of the Japanese view of sex? And despite parental scolding, children romp about freely and play games in the tub——a reflection of how Japanese raise their children these days, lively and a little naughty?

The old men seem to regain their youth as they submerge themselves in the hot water, chatting about the good old days. I hear that the suicide rate among the elderly in Japan is very high, but I cannot help doubting the statistics, observing them as I do, forever cheerful and contented-looking, at the sentô.

But the scene which most captures my fancy is that of parent and child washing each other's back. The normally stern, reproving father gently scrubs his son, and the boy, probably a little rogue anywhere else, respectfully washes papa's back. I feel I am witnessing what it really means to be a family, and the scene gives me a warm, tender feeling. The "generation gap" does not exist here. And that is why I love the sentô.

Wood-hung Lee

Nawanoren, 縄のれん

——A small drinking place (lit.
"rope curtain").

Several years ago, as part of a sociological experiment, I worked for a few weeks on the production line of a smallish factory in the Osaka area. Much to my delight, my fellow workers accepted me warmly and seemed to enjoy talking to this novel part-time worker who had suddenly appeared in their

midst. Before long I was invited to stop off on the way home from the factory for a drink; this was my first encounter with those unique, little Japanese pubs called *nawanoren*.

Many times that summer we stopped off on the way home from work. We would stop in tiny nooks sometimes big enough for just six or seven people, always greeted by a loud, cheerful *irasshaimase* which, with the Japanese male's penchant for slurred articulation, often sounded to me like a totally unarticulated shout, though a friendly one.

Now when I hear the word nawanoren many happy images come to mind——images of warm welcomes, the coziness of small, friendly places, the taste of hot sake on a windy January night, or of ice cold beer on a steaming August night, and an array of tasty treats that go well with those beverages.

A *noren* is a small curtain that hangs down part way from the top of the door outside many types of small shops, but most especially the doors of small eating and drinking places. *Nawa* looks somewhat like rope and is made from a hemp-like straw substance. Usually the word nawanoren is used in a transferred sense, however, and refers to a special type of small Japanese tavern or pub. In a nawanoren the main stress is on drinking, usually sake, but also beer; and recently you will see whiskey on hand for those of more refined taste. The food is simple: perhaps *o-nigiri* (rice balls), *shioyaki* (fish coated with salt and roasted), various kinds of *sashimi* (thinly sliced raw fish), and many, many more varieties. At one of my favorite spots near where I live, I like to order the broiled head of a fish called *hamachi*. It is called by different names in different parts of Japan, but, at any rate, it is something like mackerel and the head broiled is delicious.

I have had some of my most interesting conversations in these tiny taverns with slightly inebriated, red-faced Japanese who usually become extremely loquacious and friendly after a few drinks. Here you can truly encounter one aspect of the heart of Japan.

Charles Hancock

Yakitori, やきとり

Pieces of chicken, marinated,
skewered and charcoal-broiled.

The *yakitori-ya* (a small eating establishment specializing in
grilled chicken) resembles in atmosphere a pub or small cafe in
the West. Unlike a Japanese bar, cabaret, or nightclub, however,
the yakitori-ya caters to the after-work crowd looking for an
inexpensive drink made all the more enjoyable when served
along with tasty morsels of chicken.

It was the delicious smell of meat being cooked over a
charcoal grill which first led me to the yakitori-ya, and when I
ventured inside, I was greeted with a hearty *irasshai*. The shop
was a tiny cubicle with room for only five or six people. Smoke
hung over all, and people noisily called out their orders.

Watching the cook deftly arrange the meat on the grill, I
noticed a certain similarity between this cuisine and the American barbeque. In both styles of cooking, the meat is basted with
a sauce and cooked over an open grill; but there the similarity
ends. *Yakitori* (literally grilled chicken or fowl, but now a
generic term applied to other kinds of meat as well, including
some internal organs of beef and pork grilled in this manner) is
served on little bamboo skewers in bite-sized portions, in accord-
ance with the Japanese preference for the small and delicate and
in contrast to the American penchant for the large and massive.
The meat itself has a uniquely Japanese flavor, having been
marinaded in *shôyu* (soy sauce) and *miso* (bean paste), both
made from the soy bean.

Since that first visit to a yakitori-ya I have made several other
interesting discoveries. I found that yakitori is sometimes
seasoned only with salt and hot pepper (in which case it is
called *shioyaki*); that the sauce varies from shop to shop, for
each establishment has its own recipe; and, finally, that the
clientele of a yakitori-ya is predominantly male——one rarely
sees an unescorted woman. Perhaps by way of compensation,
many poultry shops as well as yakitori-ya operate small grills

facing the street for the benefit of housewives making their daily rounds of shopping.

The influence of the English language is apparent in the names of various kinds of meat served at a yakitori-ya: the Japanese order *reba*, *hatsu*, and *tan* for liver, heart, and tongue. This fact seems to indicate the urge of the Japanese to adopt what is foreign only to alter it to make it conform with their indigenous culture.

Yakitori-ya are to be found throughout the country: simply let your nose be your guide.

Shirley Miyasaki

Demae, 出　前
The delivery of prepared food.

I had not been in Japan for long before I had occasion to make use of *demae*, the meal-delivery service offered by nearly all inexpensive restaurants, and to marvel at its speed and convenience. Demae could have originated only in a land such as Japan where tradition places great importance on personalized service, and thanks to it a quick meal——for unexpected guests at home or for oneself when either too busy to leave the office or just not in the mood to cook——is no further than the telephone. The meal arrives warm on the plate along with a pair of wooden chopsticks, or in the case of Western-style food, with knife and fork wrapped in a paper napkin. Freed from the burden of cooking a meal or even from having to go out and get it, one is at liberty to work uninterrupted at the office or to entertain properly one's guests.

The streets and lanes of every Japanese city around noon and evening are filled with young restaurant workers in white shirts and caps pedalling hurriedly on their bicycles to deliver orders, balancing several stacked trays in one hand while steering with the other. Still more ride on motorcycles equipped with special load racks designed to carry even the soup without spilling a drop. The deliverymen do not leave you with dirty dishes, either; they will return to clear the table and collect the bill.

Sadly, the pace of modern life is forcing the demise of this system. In former times a restaurant would deliver at no extra cost the most meager of orders at any time it was open for business, but now many places will turn down an order for just a sandwich, especially if it comes at an odd hour, and are apt to charge a small fee even when they are in the mood to deliver. These changes reflect the rising status of the laborer in Japan, and although I have no reason to oppose this trend, I still have special places in my heart and stomach for the diligent shops that deliver free of charge a piping hot meal and take away the plates before the sauce has dried on them. I cannot swear that the extra care really makes any difference in the taste, but it is these shops, all the same, which claim my loyal patronage.

Mareile Onodera

Kissaten, 喫茶店
A coffee shop or tea parlor.

Above all the *kissaten* is a symbol of civilized living. A necessary haven from the insane bustle that is modern Japan, it offers alcoholic drinks as well as coffee, tea, cocoa, and an assortment of abominable soft drinks. But it is not a bar; the coffee shop harbors no hustling bar girls and no overfriendly drunks. And it is free of that air that urges one to drink in the Japanese bar as though racing against some invisible and invincible clock.

The bar is designed for commercial love-seeking, for hankypanky, while the *dôhan* (couples) coffee shop offers the grounds for testing the new "way of romantic love." And while the bar habitué goes to his favorite drinking spot to find (or escape from) a mistress, a mother substitute, or just a sympathetic ear, the coffee shop customer often wants only to drop out of all that, to sit in peace, listening to music, reading, or conversing with congenial people.

Most large office buildings house one or more kissaten which serve as offices away from the office (and from the boss's scrutiny). For many free-lancers, the kissaten is their only office. As an office, the kissaten offers the relaxed ambience conducive to that oh-so-gentle feeling out essential to Japanese business.

And it is this ambience that recommends it for casual dates, and even occasionally for the meeting that is the first step toward an arranged marriage.

Japanese housewives cultivate flower arranging but not the arts of arranging a guest list or making party conversation, and many of them fear being looked down on for the cramped quarters they inhabit. Consequently, they avoid entertaining at home, and the kissaten offers an ideal solution for light entertaining or as the place to go after dining out.

Nowadays kissaten are to be found in rustic villages that have been transformed into ski or bathing resorts. They prosper three floors below ground in shopping arcades, and at the top of

smog-bound skyscrapers. They are everywhere——as they should be.

Rivalry between kissaten is intense (there were 7177 as of Dec. 1974 in Tokyo alone) so that each one strives to provide an atmosphere different from its jostling neighbor's. Often it is the coffee itself that is the main difference, and a number of shops induce customers inside with rare types or special blends. With increasing internationalization has come coffee connoisseurship, a game the Japanese play with a restrained flair. But it is usually the music and decor that attract customers.

In their rush to modernize, and out of their passion for austerity, now moribund, the Japanese have largely ignored the convenience of the public bench. And since squatting by the roadside is an embarrassing vestige of less self-conscious times, a major attraction of the kissaten is a seat. Ahh, the luxury of simply being able to sit down!

For the next hedonistic advance, I propose cleaning up the smog and, weather permitting, moving the kissaten outdoors. There lies an even higher peak of civilization.

Ronald V. Bell

Hosutesu, ホステス
Japanese pronun. of "hostess,"
meaning bar or cabaret girl.

One does not notice them during the day but at night signs blare out their message with unusual clarity. With similarities to both the gaudy night clubs of the West and Japan's own refined geisha and teahouses, a vigorous new hybrid has developed in the form of the cabaret. Catering to large numbers of businessmen it can be viewed as the recreational wing of Japan's corporations. Its main source of attraction is the *hosutesu*, hired for the specific purpose of entertaining men.

Actually the hostess is many things. She is a pamperer, a teaser, a counselor, but most important she is a woman who makes herself available to men so that they may relax and enjoy themselves. She may offer just the right mood for business negotiation that would be difficult in the more formal realms of the office. Or she may simply provide the means for a man to escape from the daily routine of his structured life and to regain his sense of being a man among other men. In another sense, she offers an amorous rapport which invites the customer to play the role of seducer. This sometimes leads to a date outside the cabaret but for the most part simply puts a little swagger back into a man's steps. She is there to make men laugh, to make them forget themselves, to give them a woman's loving attention which is so important. This is her job and it is how she earns a living.

The Japanese wife tolerates this largely because this is what society expects her to do. Because of the seemingly respectable nature of cabarets she is usually more upset about uneaten dinners and money spent than about suspected infidelity.

There are many reasons why a girl might become a hostess but essentially the big temptation is money. For a single girl away from home without any technical training the economic prospects are quite slim. Thus the cabaret offers such girls the means to support themselves with a little glamour thrown in. If the girl likes it she may make it her livelihood even though it may prove a handicap in finding a good husband. For a girl it's a chance, but for such girls there aren't many other kinds of chances in Japan.

Robert Wallace

Chippu, チップ

Japanese pronun. of "tip,"
meaning gratuity.

This is the Japanese pronunciation of the English "tip," the meaning in both cases being "gratuity." It is perhaps typical of Japan that it would have the word while, at the same time, remain relatively innocent of the custom. Indeed, in the manner of most foreign words entering the language, it has ceased to mean what it means in the West. The word in Japanese implies something given for something received. It does not imply, as it does in the West, a custom which rewards people for doing nothing at all. The *chippu* is as occasional and as deserved in Japan as it is habitual and unwarranted in the West.

Something given for something received——this is the important phrase in Japan, the land of quid pro quo. At the same time, however, though a chippu is given when something out of the ordinary is received, waitresses, taxi drivers, doormen, etc., do not feel that their customary services represent anything out of the ordinary. This is their work. They are paid for doing it. To charge patrons simply for doing their job is unthinkable to most of them.

At the root of this (and——put conversely—— at the root of tip-grubbing in the West) is the pride taken in doing a job well. A tip implies that you are not doing your job, that you must be bribed into doing it. The Western attitude, on the other hand, that a tip is deserved and that the customer may risk verbal abuse if he does not leave one is based, I think, not upon such a feeling of pride but upon its abject opposite.

In Japan extra help or service, then, should be met with a chippu, which is only fair since its performance is not among the duties of the receiver. This is as true for the hoisting of heavy trunks as it is for the loan of sexual favors. But this is only one kind of chippu. Others consist of money given before anything is asked——doctors and lawyers are familiar with this form——or of monthly or annuál "reminders" to keep the extra service coming, etc. But, in whatever form, the economic basis is much sounder than the foreign tip-system. In Japan, something real is paid for.

Donald Richie

O-miyage, おみやげ
A souvenir, usually in the form
of present or gift.

O-miyage, literally a product native to a certain region, is
usually given to someone as a memento of the place and the
time one has been enjoying with another. Surely no foreign
visitor to Japan leaves without some sort of o-miyage. It is
always a pleasant surprise, although——to the visiting foreigner
at least——it is sometimes given seemingly for no reason, other
than as a sign of respect or deference.

Until recent times Japanese lived in small communities under
severe conditions and were dogged by calamities, natural and
otherwise. People celebrated not only their personal joys but also
the joy of the community when it overcame troubles and
hardships. They strove for a kind of kinship through sympathy
with each other's trials. This communal feeling is behind the
custom of giving presents or money to friends and acquaintances
before a wedding or funeral. With a wedding gift one wishes a
young couple well at the start of their married life, and with a
funeral gift one assists the bereaved family in conducting a
proper ceremony. In either case the gift helps to lighten the
financial burden imposed by a wedding or funeral, but in the act
of giving there is something more: it reaffirms among those
involved a sense of community.

It is not uncommon to give presents to persons going abroad
or even to young students going on brief excursions within
Japan. This custom originated at a time when traveling conditions were so harrowing that one who set out was sometimes
never to be seen again. If the traveler did return safely, however,
he would inevitably present those who had given him farewell
gifts——as he still does today——with o-miyage.

The traveler also brought back *miyage-banashi*, the experiences on a journey he told to friends back home. Those who
sent a traveler off eagerly looked forward to such tales upon his
return and listened with gratitude, as if they were indeed a kind
of gift. But now miyage-banashi have lost much of their former

appeal, having been upstaged by pictorial magazines and television.

Japanese are in the habit of taking along some small gift (called *te-miyage*, or simply o-miyage) when they pay their friends and relatives a call, reciprocating in advance the anticipated hospitality of their hosts. And when they leave for home, their hosts will often turn around and present them with some o-miyage in return.

The Japanese thus exchange gifts seemingly *ad infinitum*, but in an age of mass-production, a growing craze for foreign-made items, and a diminishing interest in crafts, the appearance, let alone the giving of the true o-miyage is becoming something of a rarity.

Fred Dunbar

Hakurai, 舶　来
Imported; foreign-made (items).

"Japanese drink the label," a foreigner sipping scotch tells TV audiences in Japan, "but I drink the contents." To any Japanese, the commercial's message is clear: why waste your money on some outrageously expensive import when you can enjoy a good, domestic brand at a fraction of the price?

The lure of items from abroad and a willingness to pay more for them is universal, but surely no people put a higher premium on imports than do the Japanese. *Hakurai* literally means "brought by ship," but *hakurai-hin* (imports) are almost invariably the products of Western Civilization. Living themselves in a hierarchical society, the Japanese tend to view the world as a hierarchy of cultures. Western diplomats and soldiers after Commodore Perry demonstrated that what was Japanese did not meet Occidental standards, and ever since the Japanese have expended enormous amounts of energy creating a facade acceptable to the West.

Today the tables have turned and the West is emulating the culture and technology of Japan, but the Japanese still have a weakness for merchandise with a foreign label. There is nothing particularly exotic about scotch, for example, even in Japan, where some very good whiskey——as well as some of the world's finest textiles, automobiles, and precision equipment, to name a few items——is made. The Japanese are perfectly aware of this fact, too, and are quick to boast of their achievements to their Western companions, especially when those achievements eclipse the Occidental competition. Yet they seem unable to quench their desire for the new, the unusual, and the foreign.

Thus, despite (or perhaps because of) the outrageous price of anything foreign in Japan, from scotch to sports cars, imports will always have their place in a society eager to maintain appearances. Hakurai-hin are prized for their decorative value; they are strictly for public consumption. While our first instinct is to hide the good bottle of scotch so that guests will not drink it

up, good (i.e., imported) scotch in Japan is definitely for show. Not only is the bottle in full view behind the guest-room liquor cabinet's glass doors, it is often flanked by an empty bottle or two. Even when drained, the bottles lose none of their power to dignify the liquor cabinet or elevate their owner's prestige.

The domestic scotch manufacturer's practical appeal to TV listeners will no doubt be in vain. The label does have taste. If there are any doubters, just ask the owners of all those empty bottles.

Edward Fowler

Omake, お ま け

An addition, a premium, an extra, something "thrown in."

Mrs. Suzuki walks into the neighborhood butcher's to buy some ground beef for the family's dinner. She notes the price ——¥150 per 100 grams——and orders 500 grams. The butcher dutifully places the ground beef on the scale. He eyes the scale ——515 grams——and then Mrs. Suzuki, who is a regular customer, and announces to her magnanimously, *Omake!* Mrs. Suzuki smiles, pays the butcher ¥750, and walks out with 515 grams of ground beef.

Most Japanese residential neighborhoods are studded with small shops, all highly competitive and all engaging to some degree in the custom of handing out omake. This custom takes several forms, such as the one illustrated above of giving a little extra of an item at no extra cost, or of giving an extra something when a customer buys an item at the list price (the butcher might throw in a tiny bottle of sauce with the meat, the dry cleaner a needle-and-thread set with the cleaning, the clothier a handkerchief with the new shirt), or of knocking the odd ten or twenty yen off the total bill.

As for determining when, how much, and to whom to offer omake, reason dictates that a shopkeeper bestow omake most willingly upon the frequent, and in particular the free-spending, customer, from whom he will reap the most profit in the long run. But reason is not the final yardstick, at least not in Japan. The custom of giving out omake is based more on the shopkeeper's frame of mind than on the price tag, and he is far more apt to favor a penny-pinching but charming customer with an omake than he is a free-spending but arrogant one. And even a foreigner such as myself might be blessed with an omake the very first time he walks into a shop, the object perhaps of the shopkeeper's proud demonstration of Japanese generosity.

Some may question the worth of omake and ask why shopkeepers bestow such needless favors as an extra 15 grams of meat when they could just as easily reduce a needlessly high price. Yet if they were to march down the street demanding an end to omake and unfair prices, few would listen. For in Japan, omake is an institution, one of the lubricants in the game of human relations, a game at which people here are extremely adept and seem to enjoy thoroughly.

Edwin Fairbank

Tachishôben, 立 小 便
To urinate (lit. "while standing")
in a public place.

Tachishôben, the act of urinating in public, is typically Japanese only in that it is performed so much more openly and freely than in most other countries. Though there are occasionally enforced laws against the practice, it is still commonly encountered and had best be regarded as a typical part of the Japanese scene.

Typical, certainly, is the process of reasoning which permits tachishôben. Traditionally, the Japanese entertain a strong dichotomy between yours and mine——or, more precisely, ours and theirs. Thus private politeness and public rudeness, and the other seeming paradoxes which have long been observed by the apprehensive foreigner. The fact that no one practises tachishôben within the private garden but everyone does on the public street on the other side of the wall, is just another example of the dichotomy at work.

The garden belongs to us, or to people we know, and must therefore be respected. The street, on the other hand, since it belongs to everybody belongs to no one and need not be respected at all. Also, the viewers of the tachishôben are either complaisant friends or else nameless strangers and, in either case, if for entirely different reasons, censure is not to be expected.

There is another reason for this indulgence. Urban Japanese still cling to their rustic origins and are fond of calling even Tokyo a village, albeit an overgrown one. They secretly yearn for the rural life of a former age and admire behavior among their fellows which they feel to be natural, just as they admire a life which is natural, i.e. in tune with nature. To them the modern urban scene is not welcome, but only tolerated. No one would take a farmer to task for urinating in a stream or at a roadside while working in the paddies, and citified Japanese, recognizing the farmer in themselves, look upon those under the influence or nonchalantly relieving themselves in the street not entirely without approval, recalling perhaps a village life that once was, a

life closer to nature and to the natural instincts of man.

Tachishôben thus joins a host of like manifestations (rowdy drunkenness in public, knocking people about in crowded trains and subways, public vomiting, breaking of queue lines, etc.) which insist that the civic ideal does not exist even though private politesse does.

In this way tachishôben enjoys a tenuous if polar link with the tea ceremony. Both, at extreme positions, are a part of the spectrum of the Japanese way.

Paul Richards

Onbu, お ん ぶ

To carry on one's back; piggy-
back.

Married to an American and living in the States, I raised my
daughter strictly in the hope that she would grow up into the
strong woman that American society demands. I was more
lenient with my boy, however, for I was determined to nurture
him into a loving, filial son. I did this for both his sake and
mine. My ideal of a man is a warm, gentle person, and I wanted
to give my son everything my mother had given me as an infant:
breast feeding, much fondling, and the security of *onbu*.

The custom of carrying a baby on one's back in Japan
probably developed as much out of necessity as motherly affection, however. A woman in former generations had many children and too much work to look after them all. By strapping an
infant onto her back, she could prevent mishaps and free her
hands for housework and shopping. Be that as it may, I determined to adapt this custom to the modern American landscape,
feeling certain that the peace of mind I gained from having my
baby close to me even while I worked would more than com-
pensate for any stares and snickers from astonished neighbors.

Far from laughing at the sight of me and my child strapped
together, my neighbors were impressed with onbu's physiological
and psychological advantages. Some of them even took to
imitating me and were soon washing dishes and trimming the
lawns with their babies strapped to their own backs. Once
during the neighborhood social hour, one of the housewives, a
former psychology major, lectured to us on onbu as being *the*
answer to people's need for skinship in our present day and age,
and another talked fondly of how much closer a mother would
become to a child she had raised on her back. It struck me then
how alone everyone in America seems to be, not just foreigners
like myself.

Each time I return to Japan I see fewer and fewer women
carrying babies on their backs and more carting them in stroll-
ers. Young mothers have grown disenchanted with onbu, partly

out of reaction to the changing times——women have fewer babies and the wealth of home appliances has greatly eased the burden of housework; partly out of fear——they think it will make their children bow-legged; and partly out of vanity——they think that having a baby slung on one's back makes them look ridiculous. But I still contend that this custom is a healthy one, not only for the baby's emotional security but for the mother's as well. It is a unique way to deepen the bond between mother and child.

Masako Ford

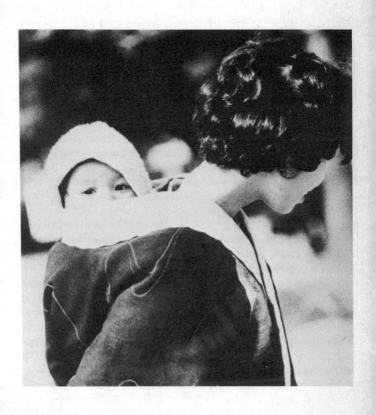

Hara, は　　ら

Abdomen, stomach; the seat
of the emotions.

The last thing I had expected to worry about when I spent a
summer in Buddhist temples was my abdomen, but the priests
instructed me during *zazen* sessions to concentrate on deriving
breath and strength from my *hara*; and when I studied *shakuhachi* my teacher told me to play the instrument not with my
mind and fingers but with my hara.

I was to learn with time that the importance of hara is not
restricted to lofty spiritual and aesthetic concerns: one's hara,
like one's heart in the West, is considered to be the center of
one's true feelings and emotions. When someone says, *Hara o
watte, hanashimashô* (lit. "Let's open our stomachs and talk"),
he is urging frank discussion; and should he "look you in the
stomach" (*hara o saguru*)——instead of in the eye——he is still
probing your real motives. The expression *hara ga ôkii* (lit.
"potbellied") means big-hearted and can be applied to persons
of any size. Saigô Takamori (1827-1877), a leader of the Meiji
Restoration and one of the great figures in Japanese history, was
in fact a large man, but the bronze statue of him in Tokyo's
Ueno Park depicts him with such a magnificent midriff that we
cannot help but be impressed by his big-heartedness.

The most important of these idioms is *haragei* (lit. "art of the
stomach") the process of feeling one another out on an issue.
The Japanese regard haragei as the highest form of interpersonal
communication. A person with a problem or in need of a favor,
unable or unwilling to confront a friend with it head on, will
merely drop suggestions; and the greater the favor, the more
allusive the suggestions. The friend, meanwhile, does not feel the
need to press for a direct explanation, but relies on his powers
of intuition. Having a common history, language, and culture,
and a rather homogeneous society, the Japanese have developed
into an art the act of communicating one's most heartfelt desires
in the fewest number of words.

If my observations on zazen, shakuhachi playing, a statue, and idiomatic expressions are not enough to convince the reader that hara is the true source of one's emotional being, let me add that tragic figures in Japan, choosing to end their lives with honor, commit harakiri (more correctly "seppuku"), plunging their swords not into their hearts, but into their stomachs.

Jane Alexandra Corddry

Oyabun, 親 分

The one in superior position in
an *oyabun-kobun* relationship.

The desire to be an *oyabun* (translated variously as boss,
leader, patron) afflicts every Japanese male I know, whether he
be company employee, government official, or local street
urchin. This desire shows itself in his almost morbid urge to foot
the bill for an outing or meal with his comrades, no matter how
hard-up for money he might be.

Being half Japanese, I can well understand this peculiar urge.
My German friends (I am also half German) have their doubts
about this practice, however. They are forever asking me what
can be gained by treating everyone. If you were in a party of,
say, four people, they argue, and paid only for your own drinks,
you could afford to drink four times as much as the Japanese
who is intent upon squandering his money on others. True
enough; but what my friends do not realize is that the Japanese
are not so much interested in their pocketbooks as they are in
bonds of emotion and obligation with others.

Western man is indeed a lone wolf——or to put it more chari-
tably, independent. It is up to the individual whether he suc-
ceeds——or falls flat on his face. But Japanese men lean on each
other more, seeking ties in the form of an *oyabun-kobun*
(patron-follower, senior-junior) relationship. I like to call this
phenomenon the "oyabun complex," for it is symptomatic of a
certain emotional weakness. Yet this heavy dependence on
others has its advantages. If a single Japanese were matched in
battle against a German, the German, I feel, would emerge
victorious. But let a hundred Japanese fight a hundred Germans,
and the Japanese would win hands down.

I personally knew a great oyabun in my judo teacher, and
although he is now dead, I still pay my respects to him by
making a yearly pilgrimage to his grave on the anniversary of his
passing. The Japanese blood which flows in me has made me
aspire to become an oyabun myself in the past; but I have no
such desire now. The reason is simple: there is no good kobun

material in today's young men, even including Japanese. It would be absurd to rule a roost of kobun who will act only when flattered, and who might betray you even then. But perhaps this is just sour grapes. The real reason may be that I simply lack the personal appeal which would qualify me as an "oyabun."

Alfred Scholz

Kaigi, 会　議
A conference, a meeting, a
convention.

In a Japanese organization, the *kaigi* takes place early and
often at all stages of decision-making, and participants may have
anywhere from substantial to peripheral involvement in the
matters up for consideration.

What is impressive about the kaigi is its sheer frequency.
Many employees spend the better part of their working day in
meetings, many of which yield no concrete results. Supplement-
ing these are informal consultations, which are an ongoing
feature of the Japanese decision-making——or rather decision-
evolving——process.

At the heart of this multi-meeting approach is Japanese problem-solving philosophy——characterized by the proverb "three
heads are better than one"——which results in overlapping
spheres of responsibility, and hence the involvement of a number of people in each phase of a decision. Since each employee
is involved in several peripherally related areas of work, good
communication skills are an essential requisite for effective
functioning.

Preceding all but the most informal kaigi are a series of
consultations carried out by the meeting's principals. These
pre-briefings are aimed at securing basic consensus even before
the issues are formally introduced in the kaigi. Successful pre-
briefings make all participants feel involved, while failure to
pre-consult may jeopardize the proposal itself.

In contrast to the still-prevalent Western practice of handing
down decisions from above, virtually all decisions in Japan are
made by those employees who are actually involved (directly or
indirectly) at the grass-roots level. When the initial proposal has
been fully scrutinized, reviewed, and modified practically
beyond recognition, it is relayed upwards, and management
meets to either stamp its approval or send the plan back for
further modification. Thanks to the copious consultations which
have taken place in and out of the kaigi, the plan——once

approved——goes into instant and coordinated application. Everyone even remotely involved has been consulted and is well educated on all aspects.

Considering the amount of time Japanese employees spend in kaigi, a Westerner might wonder how they ever get down to work. The point is that communicating and consulting with one another is the *essence* of their jobs. Japanese organizations stress such interaction as the surest means of developing foolproof, coordinated plans of action. In fact, the kaigi is a major medium of the Japanese organization's pivotal plus: the well-developed communication habits of employees and a firmly ingrained teamwork, grass-roots approach to problem-solving.

Katharine L. Day

Keiyaku, 契 約

A contract, compact, or agreement;
also, an understanding.

The translation of *keiyaku* as "contract" seems appropriate in legal terms in that Japanese contracts do not differ radically from those in Anglo-American law. Contracts concerning real estate, patents, trademarks and licenses are specific much in the manner of Western practice. Moreover, since the late nineteenth century Japanese legal structure has been patterned after that of the West.

A Westerner coming to Japan with this limited information may have distinct expectations as to how people should behave in circumstances involving contracts. With unshaken faith in principles often abstracted from reality and rights conceived to be self-evident, one might pugnaciously plunge into confrontations only to be met with a pragmatic notion articulated in the phrase "case by case."

Personally, I view keiyaku as a "contingent principle" in that drawing up a contract may be manifest binding of a pre-existing relationship, and the execution of the contract terms may be tolerated as contingent upon varying circumstances to a greater degree than in the West. In fact the tenet of "changed circumstances" is applied frequently. Rather than imposing principles on a relationship, interpersonal dynamics may generate the principles to be applied and serve as mitigating factors if one party fails to perform. It is not unusual to have considerable modification of existing contracts although some "basic contracts" are sufficiently ambiguous so as to allow for extremely flexible interpretation.

This pliant conception of keiyaku may be a partial reflection of human interaction in Japan with emphasis on interpersonal understanding (frequently nonverbal), harmony and conciliation perhaps reached more intuitively than by rigorous logic. Keiyaku as a legal term creates the concept of rights and obligations which, however, may be more apparent than real. Rather, in keeping with traditional behavioral patterns is the notion of duty to the requisites of the established relationship. In this connection we find a marked tendency to settle disputes out of court, sometimes through direct negotiations or with the help of a mediator. To press for litigation and reject conciliation and compromise is yet considered scandalous and may be highly detrimental to one's future transactions. Thus in Japan in 1963 more than half of all civil cases (presumably many involving contracts) were resolved by mediation instead of judgment as opposed to extensive litigation in the United States. This leads me to believe that, with regard to contracts in Japan and the United States, we are dealing with rather different conceptual schemes and notions of "reality," with interpersonal relations in Japan being the more tangible "reality" than "principles."

Anne Elizabeth Murase

Meishi, 名　刺
A business card, a calling card.

Possession of a *meishi*, the central prop in the act of self-introduction, is imperative for anyone in the business or professional worlds in Japan. Without a meishi to present, a Japanese feels unequipped for meeting new people. By not presenting a meishi, one is not only breaching etiquette but also risking being forgotten.

A meishi gives (in the order it is read) the name of one's organization, rank therein, one's own name, and the address of the organization. Thus, even an untitled Mitsubishi employee commands respect by virtue of his company's name, while an employee of a small, obscure firm——even though an executive ——may not necessarily be accorded similar respect.

A meishi is as good as a person's word, and can serve as a receipt or even as an introduction to a third party when its owner merely jots down on it the oft-used phrase, "Please take care of this person" (i.e., the bearer of the card); for this reason people with power and position hand out their meishi with great discretion.

The actual exchange of meishi might take place as follows:

Messrs. Suzuki and Tanaka, both employees in highly respected banks, are introduced to each other briefly at a party. Each immediately pulls out his meishi.

Suzuki (carefully handing over his meishi so Tanaka can read it as given to him and bowing simultaneously): I'm happy to make your acquaintance.

Tanaka (similarly handing over his meishi while bowing at a slight angle to avoid collision): The pleasure's mine. (The two men pause to examine each other's cards.)

Suzuki (impressed): Ah, I see you work at your bank's main branch.

Tanaka (seeing that Suzuki works for Mitsui at a Nagoya branch office): That's right. Say, isn't this a coincidence. My brother-in-law's cousin, Ito by name, was stationed up till last

June at Mitsui's Nagoya branch. You wouldn't happen to know him, would you?

The conversation continues, a common basis for association having been established. Later, the two men add each other's meishi to their burgeoning collections. Mr. Tanaka knows that he just might have occasion to call on Mr. Suzuki's assistance should he ever need something done at Mitsui——and vice versa.

Katharine L. Day

Bônasu, ボーナス
Japanese pronun. of "bonus,"
meaning wage- or salary-bonus.

A dictionary definition of bonus: something given or paid over and above what is due; a sum of money given to an employee over and above his regular pay, usually in appreciation for work done.

A newcomer to Japan once remarked: "The Japanese must be extremely hard workers. They all get bonuses, not just once a year, but twice a year." However, the Japanese meaning of *bônasu* is not the same as described in the above definition or illustration. In Japan a bônasu is part of a worker's regular pay that is held by the employer and then given to the worker in a lump sum twice a year. These bonuses, usually given in June and December, are equal to a large part of a worker's entire salary for the year. Psychologically it seems to the worker like a true bonus. If you ask him how much he makes he will usually quote his monthly salary only and not average in the bônasu.

The seniority system, lifetime employment, and loyalty to one company predominate in the Japanese business world. The merit system and job mobility are not common. Salaries, bonuses and promotions are determined almost entirely by the year that the worker begins his employment. His loyalty to only one company is usually ensured by the fact that he cannot transfer his seniority to another company. The merit system, although weak, appears to a small degree in the amount of bonus received by workers of equal seniority. Some may receive slightly more or slightly less than others depending on how their work has been evaluated.

The bônasu serves many useful functions in Japanese society. For example, June and December are the traditional gift-giving seasons and department store and shops are crowded with customers. Banks also receive a part of this tremendous sum of money in the form of savings. This semiannual boost to the economy has a great effect on the nation and on the individual. The psychological feeling of a worker when he receives, all at once, an amount of money equal to three or four times his monthly salary is quite exhilarating, much more so than if he received no bônasu but a higher monthly salary. The aforementioned are some of the advantages of the Japanese bônasu system.

There are disadvantages also. One would be that employers withhold a portion of each worker's salary and keep it for rather long periods, meanwhile being able to use the money which rightfully belongs to the worker. The same argument has been used regarding the withholding tax. In spite of this and other disadvantages the advantages would seem to outweigh them for the average Japanese. In Japan today one would find very few opponents to the bônasu system.

Albert W. Peterson

Banzai, 万　歳
Exclamation, meaning "hurrah,"
or "hurray."

Banzai is the spicy word that invariably seasons war tales and comic strips in the West about the Pacific war. In a typical scene, a kamikaze pilot, the sweat streaming down his face and a band with a red rising sun tied round his forehead, bellows out a barbarous "banzai!" the instant before he crashes his fighter plane into an enemy ship. Even today, that ferocious cry is indissolubly linked with many Westerners' image of wartime Japan and her presumably bellicose people, and along with geisha and harakiri it is one of the few Japanese words to enter the Western vocabulary.

This notion of banzai, however, is but another misconception Westerners have concerning things Japanese, and most of us are astonished to learn that banzai is a word which not only predates the Japanese language (it is of Chinese origin) but whose meaning ("may you live for ten thousand years") is surprisingly benign. Thus, while many know the word as a battle cry, few are familiar with its use in peacetime. A few years ago I accompanied a friend of mine from Tokyo by train to Nagoya, where a teaching post at the same university I work at was waiting for him. No sooner had we set foot on the platform at Nagoya station, however, than we heard a thundrous cheer of "banzai!" reverberate three times in succession from the neighboring platform where a Tokyo-bound train was due to leave. My friend stopped cold in the midst of the bustling, pushing crowd, stared open-mouthed at the other platform, and finally asked me jokingly but with a curious glint in his eye, "Don't tell me those people over there are going to . . . ?"

Before I could answer, an elderly Japanese gentleman, amused by the utterly puzzled look on my friend's face, walked up to us with a sympathetic smile and informed us that the group on the far platform was seeing off a colleague who was transferring to the Tokyo branch——which is to say the main branch——of his company, and that the occasion called for a triple banzai to

congratulate him on his promotion (a move to the capital was definitely a move upward) and to wish him good luck at this most auspicious juncture in his career.

My friend seemed only half convinced at this explanation, however. As we walked down the stairs out of the station, he exclaimed that it was beyond him why anyone would go to Tokyo to the accompaniment of a war cry.

Jean-René Cholley

Dantai, 団　体
A group, usually with nuance of
all members from the same source.

Dantai means group, but it lacks the connotation of casual
gathering that "group" has. To a degree not even hinted at in
the English equivalent, dantai is an institution: just as the
individual is the lowest common denominator of society in the
West, so is the dantai in Japan.

The ubiquitous bus-load of Japanese tourists is the most
blatant manifestation of this institution outside Japan. Watching
the cluster of dark suits swarm before cathedral or monument
for the group picture, one senses the dantai to be a self-suffi-
cient world less concerned with taking in the landscape than
with preserving its identity in a strange environment. Even when
traveling in their own country, however, the Japanese flock
together. Secure in their own society, members of a dantai make
no effort to mix with outsiders. A strong, familial bond exists
within the group (composed of mutual acquaintances linked by
a common profession, school, or locale), and in a sense, the
members never leave home. A Japanese can survive an alien
environment if he is surrounded by familiar faces.

Given the internal cohesion of a dantai, group-conscience——
more than self-motivation or rules——dictates an individual's
actions. A person's judgments and moral decisions are not
entirely his own; individual responsibility diffuses into group
responsibility. In return for the group's patronage, a member
offers total allegiance. Loyalty is indeed the supreme virtue. If
no one in the group stands out, neither is anyone brushed aside
or overlooked. How appropriate that Chûshingura, that most
popular of Japanese dramas, has not one or two but forty-seven
heroes.

Group loyalty and hierarchical society have a somewhat
feudal ring to Western ears, but the most superficial look at
Japan today tells us that the country is no medieval anach-
ronism. The dantai is as dynamic as it is drab. Its philosophy of
achievement through strict observance of the group's will has

been a driving force behind Japan's modernization. In Japan, numbers beget not only security but results. It is of course no secret that Japanese work well in groups. But the fact is they also learn, play, fight, and die well in groups.

The idea of paying for security with conformity may be distasteful to the Western ego. But conformity and identity need not be mutually exclusive, as any Japanese will tell you with a smile. When Descartes wrote, "I think; therefore, I am," he gave the Western world its classic definition of individual identity. Had the philosopher been brought up in Japan, he might well have said, "They think; therefore, I am."

Edward Fowler

O-miai, お 見 合

An interview or meeting with a
view to marriage.

Marriage in Japan arranged through the *o-miai*, or interview
between prospective partners, is the target of constant criticism
by Westerners. Serious-minded souls wonder what ultimately
becomes of these "marriages of convenience," while those more
sentimentally inclined wonder how such pairs, coupled as they
were without love, could ever get along. These well-intentioned
people have forgotten, however, the long tradition of pre-
arranged marriages in some European countries; even nowadays
it is not rare for well-meaning parents to invite a promising
graduate of some elite university for a Sunday afternoon coffee
when their daughter just happens to be at home.

Most young Japanese today prefer a love-match and resent
parental interference in their personal affairs; yet many still feel
more secure when their cool-headed father or mother takes the
trouble to check a prospective mate from every angle. And
besides, love is not always a prerequisite to a successful marriage; many of our grandparents got to know each other only
after they were married but were probably just as happy with
their common life as we are.

For all the good points of such marriages, the first interview
between prospective groom and bride must be an awkward
moment, and for this reason hotel lobbies are the scene of some
very amusing pantomimes. The young lady casts a flitting glance
at her prospective husband as the two exchange bows. Thereafter
she averts her eyes and affects an unconcerned air as the parents
on either side do all the talking.

It is perhaps a sign of the times that the young man often
looks more embarrassed than the lady. He nervously fingers his
necktie or cigarette, trying desperately not to appear silly. I
know a young man who has achieved a certain expertise in
"o-miai watching." He claims that he can tell in less than five
minutes whether or not the two principals have a future, and
even whether or not either has had previous o-miai experience.

Since his own two experiences with o-miai ended in failure, he has resolved to master the "technique," as he puts it, before attempting it a third time.

Jean-René Cholley

Sumairu, スマイル
Japanese pronun. of "smile."

"A smile is just a frown turned upside-down," goes a current pop hit. Had the lyricist perhaps spent some time in the mysterious Orient? A Japanese businessman dashes for a train, only to come up seconds late; the greengrocer informs you that he has no good tomatoes today; a student makes an embarrassing mistake in the classroom: common scenes of everyday life in the city. In Japan, however, these people do not show an expression of regret, disappointment or embarrassment; more probably, in

the place of a frown, grimace or whatever else would seem appropriate, there is a smile. An imperturbable, even cheerful smile.

Why are they smiling? The reasons may be buried deep in the Japanese psyche, but few would claim that the smile is felt, or, if felt at all, is connected to any emotion which a Westerner would associate with smiling. And this is the point here: the Japanese smile, when it signifies anything at all, is often a sign of embarrassment, regret, discomfort, or even anger.

If one looks around a bit, innumerable examples of this seeming phenomenon may be discovered. Even Buddha——what is he smiling at? Inscrutable? Certainly. But, it may be, deliberately so. Japanese readily admit that they are taught from childhood to be conscious of their place in the social order and to repress the stronger emotions. Since total repression is obviously unhealthy, if not downright dangerous, it may be that the smile was hit upon as a kind of mask for such feelings. A safety valve, if you will. Whatever the reasons, and even considering that Westerners may find such a system by turns maddening, baffling, or sometimes insulting (one's rudimentary Japanese may be met with guffaws), they should bear in mind that it seems to work remarkably well for the Japanese. Surely, few people in the world are easier to get along with on a casual basis (in a train or bar, for example). And, the occasional hoot notwithstanding, they are wonderfully tolerant of others' quirks and blunders.

There are distinct advantages for the uninitiated. What traveler, walking into a strange bar or club to escape the devils of the rush hour, has not known the pleasure of being greeted as if he were an old friend, no matter how bone-weary the master of that shop might be? After a few such experiences, even the most crevice-minded foreigner may find himself, after, say, turning over his beer glass, producing one of those enigmatic upside-down frowns.

Thomas Walker

Sumimasen, すみません

Term expressing apology or gratitude.

According to every Japanese language textbook or dictionary, *arigatô* is the word a Japanese uses to express his thanks, while *sumimasen* is the word he uses to tender apologies for something (stepping on someone's toes in a crowded train, for example) about which he feels sorry. Since the latter word matches seemingly to perfection the "excuse me" of any Western language, the lazy foreigner tends to be satisfied with this definition and to look no further. Thus many a Western visitor to Japan with a knowledge of Japanese picked up in his own country experiences a mild shock when he hears a Japanese who has just had his cigarette lit by a stranger, for example, thank him with a sumimasen instead of the expected arigatô.

Logic tells us that there is no need to feel sorry for getting what we want, and it is only by stretching our imagination that we see the word as an apology for prevailing on someone who is, after all, an utter stranger. Yet even this interpretation does not seem to fit the finer nuances of the word. I can recall being puzzled a few years back by an amiable and garrulous butcher whom I patronized almost daily, for each time I made for the door after paying him, the butcher never failed to see me off with a resounding stream of these apologetic thank-you's: "Sumimasen, sumimasen!" I did not understand at first why he should be sorry that I had bought his meat until it dawned on me one day that he could be apologizing for the outrageous price of his steaks, or even thanking me for the trouble I was taking to fatten his wallet and enable him thus to purchase a new car shortly after I became one of his regular customers.

Several years in Japan have awakened me, however, to the fact that the Japanese feel very strongly about obligations to others, and that this feeling permeates their vocabulary. By saying sumimasen, one acknowledges that one has not yet properly reciprocated another's kindness. Patronizing a shop or even lighting a cigarette for somebody else can be considered as

favors which demand compensation. Arigatô translates into any language easily enough as "thank you," but sumimasen is best savored in the original.

Jean-René Cholley

Keigo, 敬　語
Words, expressions and inflec-
tions indicating respect.

When I first heard of the Japanese use of honorifics (one
aspect of that grammatical complex of polite word usage called
keigo) I was no older than my young son is now. Unlike him,
however, I did not know a word of the language.

My mother had just read a translation of a Japanese short
story and turned to my father, saying: "The courtesy of the
Japanese is simply unbelievable." My father, who was an admirer
of Japan, said: "They're certainly more polite than we are."

"But there is a limit," said my mother. "They are polite to
just everything. Here the moon is called 'Mr. Honorable Moon.' "
My father shook his head and said: "I don't know Japanese.
Maybe it's the translation, trying to be exotic."

Since then many years have passed. No translator now would
attempt to literally indicate an honorific, and exotic intent has
long given way to linguistic knowledge. Nonetheless, Western
students of the language still have difficulty finding their way
through the intricacies of keigo, and proffered explanations are
not always helpful.

"It's incredible," said my wife after reading an essay on the
peculiarities of Japanese. "Why there seems to be an infinite
number of terms for even such a simple word as 'I.' It all seems
to have to do with respect and one's own position in respect to
that of the other."

Though the terms are finite rather than otherwise one can
recognize her astonishment. The famous dictionary of syno-
nyms, *Nihon Ruigo Daijiten*, lists almost one hundred twenty
ways of expressing "I." Fortunately the majority are obsolete,
literary, or very seldom used. And, indeed, Japanese is not alone
in this peculiarity. Think of the Italian *tu*, *voi*, *lei*, the German
du and *Sie*, the French *tu* and *vous*. Still, Japanese wins in
number alone.

I reassured her by observing that one could manage quite well
with only half a dozen, used with the right person at the right

time and in the right place. My attempt was not too successful. A mastery of keigo means that not only must you know the words but you must also know how, when, and if to use them. Actually, I continue to share my wife's dilemma. It is my by now bi-lingual son who is the complacent one.

Domenico Lagana

Aisatsu, 挨　拶
——Greetings, salutations.

One of the most puzzling and problematic aspects of life in Japan for Westerners is, sadly, their inability to communicate with Japanese in the spoken language, to say nothing of being literate. The Japanese written language possesses a fierce reputation that makes strong men weep at even the thought that they might ever have to learn it. And with good reason, since even a Japanese is not fully able to read a newspaper until he has completed high school.

The spoken language, though difficult and complicated, is not impossible, and an ever-increasing number of Westerners are attempting to learn it. However, even for those who eventually are able to operate more or less comfortably in Japanese, *aisatsu*, or formal greetings, pose one of the greatest obstacles to the sensible conducting of daily life.

For every specific social relationship, there is a set pattern of what one is expected to say. This has brought about a certain inflexibility of language, resulting to some extent in social immobility. To a Japanese, trained subliminally from childhood in language usage and nuance, it is always possible and often necessary to be able to place oneself and the person to whom one is speaking in a relative position——whether it be superior, inferior, or equal——merely by listening to the way one says, "How do you do?"

These unique aisatsu, which occur in every conversation, clearly define a person's status and level. From the fishmonger who cries, *Irasshai* ("Welcome, come on in") to the society lady who, on first meeting, says, *Go-kigen yô* ("I presume you are well"), one immediately and automatically makes a mental note that will color all future dealings with the new acquaintance. There is nothing unacceptable about either greeting, but to a Japanese, it would simply be inconceivable for the fishmonger to say "Go-kigen yô." Although much has been said in the popular *My Fair Lady* about the way the English language marks

people's status, the mastery of the Japanese language and its aisatsu holds enough challenge to keep even Prof. Henry Higgins bewitched, bothered and bewildered for years.

Norman H. Tolman

Enryo, 遠　慮
Reserve, diffidence, hesitation, restraint, abstention.

A Japanese friend visits you. You offer him a drink. He may refuse by saying gently "Never mind" or firmly "Oh, no thank you. I'm not thirsty." But neither type of refusal expresses his real desire. Such is the custom of *enryo* in Japan. If you are serious about your offer, you must dismiss his objections as you mix and hand the drink to him.

About ten years ago, after I'd been here for some years already and was well aware of the meaning of enryo, I received a call from an acquaintance who wanted me to come to dinner. How I met him isn't important, but he considered our friendship stronger than it really was. After all, he had invited me to his wedding and had even presented me with a very large portrait of himself and his wife. Then, of course, I'd been to his house on several occasions for dinner and had even had a bath there once. So you can see why he considered the bond between us rather secure.

For my part, however, I found the constant invitations to dinner a bit tiresome, particularly because his home was in a somewhat inconvenient location requiring more than an hour's travel and several changes of trains. He didn't realize this and thought I was being very true to the form of enryo with my constant refusals. Well, one can refuse constant beckoning for only so long. I accepted and a date and the time was set. There was one thing that I tried to make clear to him——I would not stay for supper. He seemingly understood after I had repeated the point several times.

The day of the visit arrived and off I went on my train ride and through the various transfers. He was delighted to see me and I attempted to match his enthusiasm. He, his wife and I had a pleasant enough afternoon talking about past times, looking at pictures and sipping Japanese tea. When it got on toward five o'clock, I announced my departure. There was an immediate outburst of protestation. Back and forth the pleadings and

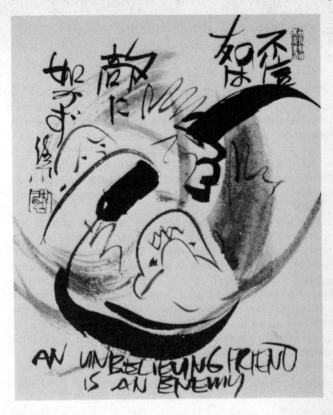

AN UNBELIEVING FRIEND
IS AN ENEMY

refusals went, until I reminded my friend of our telephone conversation. "And besides," said I, "I have another engagement for this evening."

Through the transfers on my train ride home I couldn't help being surprised that he would have gone ahead with dinner plans in spite of my assuring him on the telephone that I couldn't stay for the evening meal. Then it dawned on me that I had really followed all the forms of enryo. At least right up until I stepped out of his house.

Richard J. Hugel

Ma, 間

Space, with the meaning
of an interval, a pause.

The Japanese have the wonderful ability to enjoy the company of friends in silence as well as sound. In fact, they sometimes seem to be able to communicate far richer meaning with a pause than with a word. This ability comes in most handy indeed when the subject being discussed is either one that the people conversing wish to keep secret from others in their vicinity, or when the word itself is too charged with explosive emotional connotation to be safely uttered at that given moment.

This practice goes along very well with the general social philosophy of Japan which can be neatly summed up in the single phrase, "Don't make waves." The whole language is structured in such a way that it is never necessary to give an overtly negative answer, which greatly facilitates this "calm surface" ideal. The positive word game is even carried to the extent that I personally have had the strange experience of giving a clear, blunt refusal to a request and finding out later that the very clarity of my statement of position on the subject had made my intentions totally incomprehensible to those involved.

The best example of this type of situation that immediately comes to mind is the time I was teaching at a university in Tokyo and wanted to quit after the first couple of years, and was unable to convince the powers that were that I was serious until the fourth year. I repeatedly informed everyone who was supposed to be in charge or interested that I wanted to quit, and stopped appearing for classes, but they kept sending me my monthly salary. They did not seem to be able to understand my intentions until, finally, out of desperation, I neglected to give the final exam or turn in the grades for a semester of classes I had not taught, and they sent me a letter of release from duties.

Thus the more one studies the language, the longer one lives in this country, and the more deeply one becomes involved in the culture, the more one begins to realize that it is not only mastery of the words, grammar and idioms that makes one an expert in life in Japan. It is equally necessary to learn the rhythms and pauses of the culture in order to achieve the proper timing to contribute to the calm surface effect. This timing, or utilization of the effective pause, is called *ma*.

Don Kenny

Hanafuda, 花　札

A kind of playing cards (lit.
"flower cards").

Some years ago when I was a student in Japan I visited some friends on one of those dreary days in early June when it seems that the rainy season will last forever. Late in the afternoon after endless cups of tea and cakes the conversation began to falter. It was really time for me to go and yet I just could not bring myself to go back out into that endless drizzle for the long walk home, so I asked, "What do Japanese do to pass the time on a day like this?"

The answer I got was that the game of *hanafuda*, a variation of a card game introduced to Japan by Dutch sailors at Nagasaki at the end of the sixteenth century, helps to relieve the bore-

dom. The name hanafuda is derived from the fact that each of the cards is decorated with a flower design. There are forty-eight cards divided into four suits of twelve cards. Each of these twelve cards represents one of the months of the year and is worth anywhere from one to twenty points.

My friend brought out a deck and taught me how to play. The cards are small, perhaps 1½ × 2 inches, and they have a curious lumpy texture which comes, I was told, from a thin layer of mud sandwiched between two sheets of paper to give the card stiffness and weight.

Another thing which caught my attention was the colorful design. A pine tree or cherry blossoms or paulownia or rainfall ——each symbolic of certain scenes of natural beauty in certain months of the year—— is drawn primarily in red, blue, and black after the style of a woodblock print. It reflects, I suppose, a form of aesthetic enjoyment peculiar to the Japanese people and how they distinguish and appreciate the different seasons of the year.

Soon we were drawing cards and throwing down suits and having an hilarious time. When another friend arrived, we invited him to play too, but the rules changed. There are more than thirty variations on the game and the players adopt any set of rules agreeable to them all. In this case the newcomer was familiar with different rules so we played by different rules.

Late that night we finally broke up our party and went home, but by then the rain had lifted and the sky was clear. It occurred to me that in this game we find today some of the exuberance and vitality of the Edo townsman. I have a deck of my own which are beautifully printed by woodblock and have hand-stencilled colors, and I still play when I have the chance.

Stephen Kohl

Irezumi, いれずみ
A tattoo, tattooing (alt. *horimono*).

Only in Japan is tattooing an art: that is, only here has the craft of pigmentation become so skilled that it becomes an act of creation; and only here does this have the artistic dimensions of a long consecutive history, a number of schools, and the continued presence of acknowledged masters.

At the same time, it has never been officially recognized. Indeed, beginning as identification for criminals, tattooing has been banned a number of times in Japan's history and was made fully legal only after World War II. Yet, despite neglect and oppression, the tattoo has both survived and thrived.

The term *irezumi* means simply the insertion of *sumi* (a kind of ink made from pressed charcoal), but there is nothing simple about the operation: it is both complicated and expensive. First, it is not a matter of biceps or forearm, but the entire back and buttocks, thighs and forearms; second, the designs themselves are pictorially complicated and are drawn first in outline and then in full color; third, the instruments used are not simple electric needles but the traditional and difficult awls and chisels. It takes determination and fortitude as well as a certain amount of money to wear a complete Japanese tattoo.

Popular Japanese belief holds that only gangsters are tattooed but this is no more true than the invariability of thus decorated sailors in the West. More often Japanese tattoo-wearers are carpenters or other craftsmen, laborers, etc. This is traditional and one of the reasons given is that these men habitually worked semi-nude and the tattoo gave the appearance of seemly dress.

Actually, the reasons for getting tattooed are as various as the tattoo patterns themselves. Among these would be superstition (tattoo as talisman), investment (until fairly recently one could sell one's skin to a tattoo museum), compensation (sexual or not) and——perhaps most common——beautification.

Despite the fact that contemporary Japan affects to despise the traditional irezumi, it remains beautiful and its creation remains an art. It reflects Japanese sensibility just as faithfully as do flower arranging and the tea ceremony, arts thought more acceptable.

Donald Richie

Sumo, 相 撲

Japanese-style wrestling.

Sumo wrestling is Japan's national sport. Six times a year tournaments are held before packed audiences, and live nation-wide television coverage give millions more the opportunity to view the grandeur and excitement. Sumo fans include a rapidly growing number of foreign residents and visitors——but why all the interest? Isn't it just another sport along with baseball, golf, and boxing, all of which are also extremely popular spectator sports in Japan? No, sumo is different for two reasons: first, it embodies the spirit and essence of Japan; second, it is a unique physical activity.

The origins of sumo date back over a thousand years, and the present style and form are several centuries old. In sumo, as in most Japanese arts, form and ceremony play a major role in creating the proper atmosphere. First-time viewers often com-plain, "Why don't they get on with the show?" But one must remember that the various ceremonies——stomping the feet, clapping the hands, throwing salt, staring at the opponent, making false starts——are part of the show, and a very essential part indeed. The pre-bout exercises have an historical value, capturing and preserving the traditions and glory of the sport, and a psychological value, for both participants and spectators, slowly building up the anticipation and excitement.

Then there is the wrestling. While the formalities preceding a match take over four minutes, the actual wrestling rarely exceeds one minute, making it one of the briefest sports in the world. The reason for this is clear: the wrestlers are not built for endurance. Foreign guide books are fond of describing the wrestlers as something akin to mastodons, but they are athletes nonetheless, albeit massive ones. Most weigh between 250 and 350 pounds, much of which is concentrated in the stomach and hips. This kind of body generates the power for pushing, an essential technique in sumo, and acts as a shock absorber enabling the wrestler to stay on his feet in spite of the opponent's strong slaps and shoves. For a wrestler loses a match not only if he is pushed out of the ring but also if any part of his body, except his feet, touches the ground. The big body does not always come naturally; it requires huge portions of food and drink——a kind of forced feeding. There are many legends about the big eaters and drinkers in sumo. One grand champion drank over fifty bottles of beer at a sitting!

But don't be fooled. Sumo is not a slow sport for fat young men addicted to food and drink. Despite his size, the sumo wrestler, a kind of modern-day warrior in Japan, possesses agility, strength, speed, and balance. And as you begin to learn and understand the numerous techniques and traditions of sumo, you will become, I am sure, an avid fan of the sport.

Thomas J. Cogan

Terebi, テ レ ビ

Contraction of *terebijon*, i.e.
"television."

The Japanese nation as a whole spends more time watching television than in any other activity except work and sleep. The average viewing time is about three hours a day——more for women and on Sundays. Inhabitants of Tokyo have a choice of seven channels broadcasting a total of over 100 hours of programmes daily. Two of these are operated by NHK, the Japan Broadcasting Corporation, which is operated as a public service and financed by a viewers' licence fee. The others are commercial stations.

Today, diffusion of television receivers throughout Japan is close to 100 per cent. Colour transmission began in 1960, and is now seen by more than half the population. Television ownership in Japan has easily outstripped that in the advanced countries of the West, even though until recently income levels and the overall standard of living were considerably lower in Japan. Television is now the primary source of both information and entertainment in people's lives. The programmes, with very rare exceptions, are always in Japanese.

It might be said that a nation gets the television, like the government, it deserves. Certainly, in Japan, the character of the television service reflects the high level of technical achievement and the heady economic boom of the post-war years, as well as the deep-seated popular respect for authority. One explicit aim of NHK is to make programmes to "raise the cultural level of the nation," and the attempt is made with all seriousness.

Specifically educational programmes are broadcast almost continuously throughout the day, mostly on NHK's Educational Channel, and these are widely used in schools. On a practical level, there are plenty of useful programmes showing how to cook or do yoga exercises. The perennial daily serial dramas attract enormous audiences, and are thought to provide an important element of continuity in the nation's life.

The service of news and documentaries is excellent and

thorough. But it studiously avoids anything interpretive or controversial in character. This reflects the overriding concern of the broadcasting organizations, especially NHK, to satisfy and not offend their vast audiences; it also speaks the absence of any established custom of open-ended public debate in Japan.

It is sometimes said that the Japanese are characteristically concerned about what others think. If so, this trait could explain the uniquely dominant position that television has assumed in Japanese society——for what surer way can there be to know what others are thinking than to keep in your own home that most lifelike picture of the world outside which appears on television?

William F. M. Horsley

Ningyô, 人　形
————A doll; a puppet.

Japanese dolls are more than mere playthings. In fact, one sometimes wonders if they are played with at all, so serious is their import, so costly their making, both in time and money. A Japanese doll, which might have taken a craftsman a year to make and is worth hundreds or even thousands of dollars, is set in a protective glass case, so that it seems almost a votive object. Indeed very simple dolls of paper or bamboo are popularly believed to have magic powers to take away evil or illness, guard little babies, or bring fair weather.

The very word *ningyô* means man-shape, reminding one that among the earliest Japanese dolls were the figures of warriors and other retainers offered at the graves of nobles in place of human sacrifices. As the aesthetic is a part of life in Japan, now as in ancient times form is life. Dolls can seem to have as much life as people, especially in Bunraku.

Bunraku is a very old art brought to perfection in the early 18th century, in which exquisite four-foot dolls are cleverly manipulated to act out subtle dramas. It takes three black-robed handlers to operate each doll, as even the brows, the eyes, and the mouth must be manipulated. To the observer, it soon seems that the spirited dolls are leading their human attendants, chafing somewhat at their slowness.

Dolls in Japan are so elegant that their possession brings prestige to their owners. The making of decorative dolls, a very old art which reached its peak in the Tokugawa period, is a pastime enjoyed by many women. Though little girls lack the skill for this refined craft, they do get to play with fine dolls once a year, on March 3, the day of *Hinamatsuri* or the Doll Festival. On that day ceremonial dolls, usually at least fifteen, are set up on tiered steps. On the top step are placed the emperor and empress dolls, and the other dolls represent members of the imperial family or various courtiers. The children drink a mild sweet sake and in a sense hold court, with

every little girl a princess to her own family. These precious dolls, inherited or purchased at great expense, having conferred their royalty on the children, are then put away carefully until the next year, lest they lose any of their magic.

Mary Evans Richie

Shamisen, 三 味 線
A three-stringed musical instrument
(alt. *samisen*).

For those determined to find equivalents for all Japanese words, the *shamisen* becomes a Japanese balalaika or banjo. True, the shamisen has three strings like the balalaika, has a parchment-covered sound-box, and is played with a plectrum like the banjo. There physical resemblances end, and it doesn't sound like either instrument. But if the translators mean that the shamisen is as purely native a Japanese instrument as the balalaika is Russian and the banjo, by way of Africa, is American, then they have a point.

The sound of the shamisen is purely, cleanly Japanese. Unlike the aristocratic *shô* and koto, early brought from China, the shamisen did not appear until toward the end of the sixteenth century, coming from the Ryûkyû islands, where it was perhaps played with a bow and the sound-box is covered with snakeskin.

In Japan, where imports are often improved upon, its dynamic power and bite were strengthened by replacing the snakeskin with catskin and striking the strings with a plectrum. It became essentially a new instrument, quickly adopted by the reciters of metrical romances and forming the basis for an entirely new style of doll theatre music and declamation called *gidayû*, which survives today. As Japan settled into the socially-stable Tokugawa era, the shamisen became the all-purpose instrument of the ordinary Japanese, indispensable to the theatre, the drinking party, the geisha, and a great variety of folk music. And it came, eventually, to have a repertoire of serious, "classical" music.

It is as impossible to describe the unique Japanese quality of the shamisen as it is to describe the impassioned physical and emotional Russian vigor of the balalaika or the hard-driving American energy of the banjo. It's clear that the shamisen has about the same range and quality as the Japanese voice, from the harsh percussive thrust of the male voice, and its falsetto, to the limpid sweetness of the female. The shamisen accompanies perfectly the coarsest drinking song or the most delicate poetry, and it moves easily from bright, flashing cadenzas to lyric quietness. Its characteristic quality is that intense bittersweet tension, sad but pleasurable, that runs throughout Japanese traditional art. The guitar is the only Western string instrument with as great versatility. But increasingly the guitar has become a deracinated international voice, while the shamisen still speaks with its distinctive native sound.

Earle Ernst

Shamisen, played by Yamada Shôtarô (right) and student

Koto, 琴

A thirteen-stringed musical
instrument.

"The *shakuhachi* calls to mind a wandering priest (or was he a
spy?), a basket over his head to preserve his anonymity, playing
a forlorn melody as an accompaniment to his lonely journeys.
The *shamisen* smells of sake and reminds one of geisha, kimono
slightly askew, and a bawdy song. But the koto, its sound
echoing forth once upon a time from the rooms of Heian
noblewomen and guiding young courtiers to their ladyloves, is
refined and elegant." So a Japanese friend of mine described the
personalities of this land's traditional musical instruments.

The koto, first brought to Japan from China in the eleventh
century, has always been for those with time to enjoy life. The
strings were originally made of silk which broke if stretched
tightly, and plectrums, attached to the thumb and first two
fingers of the right hand, were made of bamboo: the combination produced a low, soft tone which made the instrument's
music most suitable as an accompaniment to the player's singing.
About six feet in length and made of hollowed out paulownia
wood, the koto is now strung with tetlon strings and played
with ivory plectrums, giving it a higher and sharper sound than
in former times. Modern compositions, moreover, have transformed it into a solo instrument requiring no little virtuosity.
During the Meiji period several schools were founded, and the
koto became popular among all classes and especially among
women, for whom it is now not only a pleasant pastime but also
one of those polite accomplishments requisite for marriage.

The sound of the koto is to me the sound of Japan, perhaps
of her innermost being. Both classical and modern pieces are
composed in the traditional three tempi——slow, moderate, and
fast. The classical pieces have no melodic line in the Western
sense. If songs are sung, the koto music follows its own theme,
creating polyphonic music rather than accompaniment.

Modern koto music is best described as sound poems. In
Nagare ("Flowing") a drop of water falls from a leaf into a

Koto, played by Tani Tamami

rivulet which grows into a stream and finally a mighty river pouring down a waterfall in a roaring cascade. In *Himawari* ("Sunflower") two koto play complementary themes which celebrate the strength and flexibility of the flower that moves to follow the sun.

In the hands of a master player, the koto pulls the listener into the music, plays on his emotions, and leaves him in silence, his spirit far removed from his surroundings.

Mary Helen Mine

Ikebana, by Adachi Tôko

Ikebana, いけ花
The art of arranging flowers.

I have been studying ikebana for almost three years now——still just a beginner. When I first came to Japan with the aim of studying a traditional Japanese art, "flower arranging," which sounded rather trivial to a student of painting and art history, was rather low on my list of priorities. So the first ikebana exhibitions I attended were exciting discoveries. Ikebana, I found, was not mere "flower arranging" (try finding an English equivalent for Kabuki or Noh) but a uniquely Japanese art of live plants. Moreover, it seemed so "modern" in its blending of an archaic animism and a sophistication developed through centuries of experimentation and theoretical speculation.

I chose to study in one of the oldest and most traditional schools, the *Ikenobô*, since it preserves the styles which developed apart from Western influence. At the beginning, along with regular classes and demonstrations, I read everything I could find on its primitive Shinto background, the influence of Taoism and of Buddhist doctrines, and the rules regarding forms and methods.

But apart from rules and reasons, the essentials of the art enter one through the fingers, hands, and muscles as well as the eyes and mind. The vast variety of materials, twigs, branches, leaves, buds, and blossoms, the forms to be created, and a sensitivity to the asymmetrical yet balanced patterns of growth in nature are initially touch and texture, a bending tension, the arching curve of a long leaf, its smooth green surface becoming a line, and that line vanishing into the memory of a distant vista —a space that is there and a space that is not. This space is an emptiness to be filled but a charged, elastic continuum where lines, surfaces, colors, space and time interpenetrate.

Though ikebana may be viewed as kind of sculpture, the "ikebanist" is not an object maker. The materials of his art are living plants and like a composer of music he is engaged in an art of duration. Whether we use one blossom in the simplest *shôka*, or great branches in the vast symbolic landscape universe of *rikka*, they are never used at their "peak of perfection" but in the bud. One of the great beauties of the art lies in an appreciation of change, the blossoming and fading. This sacrificial and sacramental use of plants is a constant reminder of the great rhythms of nature and the archaic religious origins of the art—a matter of life and death and renewal, a process which leaves no immortal masterpieces behind.

Ikebana is perhaps the clearest single expression of that appreciation of perishability which Lafcadio Hearn called "the genius of Japanese civilization." For me, the serious study of ikebana "from the inside," the involvement with aesthetic values and methods so different from those of the culture in which I was raised, has not only transformed my own feelings and ideas about art and nature, but, perhaps more significantly, has had and continues to have a profound and intimate effect on my daily life.

Joseph Lapenta

Bonsai,
盆　栽
—A potted, dwarfed tree or plant.

Pine bonsai, from the collection of Kitamura Takuzô

Bonsai, the art of raising miniature trees in shallow pots, is an offshoot of the art of gardening, which, like so much of Japanese culture, has its roots in China. Gardening in China provided more than recreation; it had a philosophical, a religious significance as well. According to the ancient Taoist attitude, one can increase one's own vitality by assembling about one's dwelling landscapes that are precise reproductions of famous sites and by collecting there precious stones, rare trees, and animals which may be considered as representative essences of the natural world. He who is able to concentrate such essences and assimilate their beneficial influence will be greatly helped on his way toward obtaining Long Life.

The Japanese, who were much influenced by Chinese thinking, early began to create such landscape gardens. Their motive in this was doubtless less religious than those of their continental models. Taoist conceptions of Immortality did not take root very deeply in Japan, where they had a more aesthetic than mystical character. Nevertheless, there is no doubt that the instinctive need which the Japanese had always felt to communicate with the natural world led them to enjoy the pleasures of landscape gardening and of the loving contemplation of little cosmoses wonderfully in harmony with their own physical and spiritual condition.

A well-known story, dating from the Heian period, concerning the minister Minamoto no Tôru (822-895), tells of an enterprise celebrated by posterity as the height of elegance and audacity in gardening. Tôru modeled the pond of the garden at his Kawara Palace in Kyoto on the landscape of the prestigious Shiogama, near Matsushima, reproducing the coasts and main islands and filling the pond with salt water, fishes, and other tiny marine animals that he procured in the sea off Naniwa (the present Osaka).

Despite the more or less legendary traditions, it would seem that the vogue of bonsai art itself began in Japan only with the Higashiyama period at the end of the fifteenth century. This art in modern times has experienced a widespread evolution. In bonsai, the focus is laid on a single, essential piece of nature, a supremely concentrated aspect of landscape, refined and scaled down to miniature proportions.

This is bonsai: the ultimate exercise in artificiality. It is nature pruned and manipulated by the human hand. But it is also an art which, like the tea ceremony or flower arranging, can lead man back to the world of nature. Gazing upon an ancient grove of stately cedars in the mountains, I have been moved by the grandeur of nature. Yet even when standing before the balanced branches of a bonsai tree in its shallow pot, I feel myself growing smaller and smaller until I have become like one of those tiny figures in an old sumi painting, contemplating deep in the mountains.

In the garden of the Imperial Palace, I once saw a pine bonsai, originally kept by the Tokugawa family; and as I looked at the split bark, the twisted branches, and the mossy trunk, I realized that the mystifying attraction of bonsai lies not in its smallness, but in its vastness.

Bernard Frank

Origami, 折り紙
Folded paper; the art of folding paper into various objects.

My first acquaintance with origami was as a second year college student when I acted as interpreter for the twenty-member Japanese handball team that played here in Czechoslovakia. Each player presented me with five examples of her handicraft, and I suddenly had an armload of one hundred origami.

Visitors to my home in Prague feasted their eyes on these delicate origami, which I had out for show. In Czechoslovakia the "art" of paper-folding is a very slipshod affair at best and limited to helmets, boats, and swallows. One does not choose any special type or color of paper, moreover, but uses newspaper or whatever else is lying around. Perhaps for this reason, then, my collection began disappearing one by one until all that remain are a precious few, which I treasure greatly.

I am seized with wonder each time I gaze at these masterly creations, for although the Japanese tend to conceive of shapes in terms of asymmetry and curve rather than symmetry and straight line, origami appears to be an exception to this aesthetic rule. In contrast to ikebana or pottery or gardening, origami has a precisely determined pattern, governed by the mechanics of folding and by a methodical, ordered construction.

One can of course find in some examples of contemporary origami (which has achieved a high level of professionalism) the development of a more abstract expression in which curved lines play an important role in the overall design. But origami, which has a tradition encompassing every kind of activity from formal ceremony (it had its beginnings in religious services) to idle pastime, is not really at home at this high, professional level: it is founded rather on the democratic proposition that anyone can learn it, simply through imitation, which fact has gained it the popularity of a folk art in Japan.

The beauty of origami's design derives from the intricate pattern of lines and paper surfaces meeting at various angles to

form an object. This pattern, aided by the tone and quality of the paper, depicts not just the object's shape but also its spiritual beauty. Being so perishable, paper cannot be used as stone is to create a monument for eternity. Paper is of the material world——the "floating world"——unable to withstand the flow of time. The idea of immortalizing such an ephemeral substance by universalizing its shape is a distinctly Oriental one.

This is why origami so appeals to me. Watching my son—— born and raised in Japan——making fold after careful fold, I have come to realize that he is not attempting to master a skill or technique that I myself lack but simply developing a sensibility quite different from my own.

Čiháková Vlasta

Shinjuku, 新　宿
District of western Tokyo developed largely after WWII.

Old Tokyo hands bemoan the decline of Shinjuku as a bohemian center. There has been, I am told, a steady encroachment by office workers upon the haunts of students, artists, and radicals. Whatever Shinjuku once was, however, the new elements and the remnants of the old still provide plenty to satisfy a great number of the usual or not-so-usual cravings.

The new is represented by the Sumitomo Building, one of the recently erected skyscrapers which may one day multiply to create somewhat of a New York skyline. That is, if the architects' presumptions about their being earthquake-proof turn out to be correct. They haven't been put to the test yet.

An earthier atmosphere prevails in the bar-lined alleys behind the slick office buildings and swank department stores. Some of the bars have decors inspired by Gorky but there is not a Bolshevik in sight, unless they are cleverly disguised in blue serge or Arnold Palmer golf sweaters. There is more singing, drinking, and staggering going on there than plotting to blow up railroad stations.

Some of the most interesting places may be the Japanese bars behind latticed doors and *noren*. For someone like myself whose imagination does not extend beyond chips and dip when it comes to something to eat while drinking, the noodles, vegetables, and fishy things served up with the sake can be a bit much. And those tiny sake cups definitely have to go. And as cozy as one of these places can be, don't expect to frequent the same one time and again. You won't be able to find it a second time.

The so-called hostess bars are best avoided. A few bottles of beer with a lady iron-butterfly can come to a staggering sum. But to give the girls their due, their self-sacrifice is inspiring; they are actually working in such places to support their aged parents, crippled brothers, or sisters in the Conservatory of Music, they tell me. Wherever you do drink, drink a lot. Then the whole bizarre Shinjuku nightlife scene will begin to make some sense.

Shinjuku, like the Left Bank or Haight-Ashbury, may be losing what it had in its heyday and may be evolving into another Ginza or Champs-Elysées, but it will always be a far cry from Peoria, Illinois.

Jack Rucinski

Kyoto, 京　都
The capital of pre-modern Japan.

One would probably need hundreds if not thousands of pages to describe even roughly this city founded more than 1180 years ago——in 794; a city which remained the capital of Japan for 1074 years (until 1868); one which even now possesses more than 1600 Buddhist temples——not to mention the hundreds of Shinto shrines.

One could, again, accumulate some statistics. This ancient

capital called Heiankyo (Peace and Tranquility) had, only a quarter-century after its founding, more than 100,000 houses and some 500,000 inhabitants. It is now, with a little over 1,400,000 inhabitants, the fifth largest city in Japan.

One could, further, mention that Kyoto is still the center of numerous Buddhist sects, that it holds the headquarters of the three main branches of the tea ceremony, that there are found the most typical schools of flower arranging.

Then there are the innumerable painters, potters, weavers, dyers, the craftsmen using lacquer, paper, wood, bamboo, and many other materials, all of whom perpetuate ancient traditions elsewhere lost. Here too were born or developed the finest traditions of Japanese music, dance, theater——from where come Noh, Bunraku, Kabuki.

If, in a few strokes, one would draw the face of Kyoto, then one would first delineate the site——a plain sloping slightly southward, surrounded by the gentle slopes of hills covered with forest and alive with the whisper of a thousand streams. Here was wisely laid the ancient capital, its vertical and horizontal avenues echoing those of the T'ang capital of Ch'ang-an.

The grid remains but, alas, under the ruthless assault of concrete, asphalt, neon, and a roaring traffic——all of them symbols of our so-called modern civilization——this old Kyoto is fading. The harmony created through the ages is dying away.

What perhaps saves it is the abundance and quality of its gardens, two hundred historically classified, thousands of others nestled in the depths of lanes and behind the most ordinary façades. Here the eye and the hand have succeeded in surrounding man and his dwellings with a space of calm and beauty. Whether it is a princely garden or that of a humble craftsman, whether it is measured in acres or in feet, the spirit of nature is here. As says the poet:

> In a stone, the mountain,
> In a grain of sand, the sea.

Jean-Pierre Hauchecorne

Sanpo, 散　歩
A walk in the sense of a stroll
or promenade.

Walking is the most universal of human activities. But to walk for pleasure is something quite different: it is a mark of the affluent society. Until the middle of the last century, Japan was the opposite——the model of a static, agricultural economy.

Japan was peopled by four social classes. First the samurai, the warrior and scholar who had no use for any form of indulgence. Next the farmer, who walked about twelve hours a day in the rice-fields and would not willingly have gone a step further. Then the artisan, who was busy turning out wares to stay above the breadline, and anyway had no social pretensions. Finally the merchant: he certainly had time to spare, but did not enjoy the formal status to go with it. Rather than parade his prosperity in public, he would take it to the gay quarters or the Kabuki theater, where the world was his own.

With the Meiji Restoration, these inflexible roles were modified. There were wild fashions in Western dress and comportment, and restrictions on movements were eased. This period saw the establishment of a middle class, and the clear separation of "work" and "leisure." The art of walking flourished.

In the present day, of course, the cities have become crowded, and the pace of life busier. Yet, behind the main roads and tall concrete buildings, in the local neighborhoods, the atmosphere of changeless calm still prevails. Of an evening, families and couples venture out, in their geta and yukata, strolling to the public bath or just taking the air. The traditional garments enforce the same peculiar gait and——especially on the feminine form——that same air of grace which was once captured in the woodblock prints of Utamaro. On Sunday the population goes further afield, to centers like Ginza, Shinjuku, or to Meiji Shrine. They wander down the streets (obligingly closed to traffic for the occasion), stopping only for an ice-cream for the children, a snapshot, or an idle moment of window-shopping.

But, sadly, this is not the whole story. The pleasure the modern Japanese takes in walking the crowded streeets on holidays may be traced, often, to the confined space of his own home, and the shortage of any parks worth the name. And during the working week, the scene is quite altered. Now it is the machines which run riot: the motor cars, the trains, the elevators, the escalators. So nowadays the citizen of Tokyo or Osaka has little time or inclination to exercise his own limbs between appointments. And his motto might be put like this: "Two legs good, four wheels better!"

William F. M. Horsley

Gaijin, 外　人
—A foreigner, an alien.

The Japanese word for foreigner is *gaijin*; the *jin* means "person" and the *gai* means "outside." Thus, on the surface the Japanese word means the same thing as the French *etranger* or the German *Ausländer*. In usage, however, something else is involved.

Neither France, nor Germany, nor any of the English-speaking countries have anything approaching the emotional nuances of the Japanese words for "insider" and "outsider." The Japanese for the former, *nakama*, implies an almost tribal closeness, an almost promiscuous degree of intimacy; the Japanese for the latter, *yosomono*, implies distance, coolness, and a degree of scorn——*mono* even when used in reference to other humans retains its original meaning of "thing."

There are many kinds of nakama in Japan, a whole nest of them. The family, the group, the school, the factory or office, the city, the prefecture, the entire country, can and do become nakama. There is, however, only one kind of yosomono and by etymological inference he has only one quality: he is unwelcome.

The foreigner thus briefed would be completely surprised by the Japan he finds, for few countries are more helpful to and friendly with foreigners. The bemused gaijin finds here a cordial helpfulness and an apparent concern that he encounters no where else. His resultant euphoria may last a lifetime——and it should because it is based upon very real qualities.

If, however, he attempts to be one of the nakama he will not succeed. His failure may embitter him. This always surprises and saddens the Japanese; they cannot understand why. To be sure a few close Japanese friends can and will but awareness of this problem is not among the national characteristics of the people. To ask a Japanese about nakama is like asking a fish about water: it is so completely taken for granted that an alternative is unthinkable. That foreigners are to be excluded and are occa-

sionally to be called mono (or other terms less polite but just as excluding) is so taken for granted that it is not even acknowledged, much less questioned.

The happy gaijin, then, is one who accepts the limits that the Japanese impose upon both his authenticity and his life in their country. The friendliness is very real, and so is the xenophobia.

Donald Richie

O-cha, お　茶

Tea. Both words ("cha" and "tea")
come from the Chinese *ch'a*.

Even in the face of the increasing popularity of coffee, soft drinks, and a beverage made of lactic acid, for the Japanese by far the most beloved of all nonalcoholic drinks remains green tea, or *o-cha*. Indeed, green tea, originally used for medicinal purposes, has long been considered so essential to everyday life that, like the terms for such other necessities as water, rice, and soy sauce, the very word itself is rarely spoken or written without an honorific prefix. Drunk scalding hot in all seasons of the year, tea has given its name to a number of things that are not exclusively connected with it. For instance, the room in the house called the *cha-no-ma* (tearoom) is actually the living room where many things aside from tea drinking take place. The *cha-ya* (teahouse) may be anything from a dealer in bulk tea to a roadside rest house to an establishment in the pleasure quarters of the past where geisha and ladies of related occupations plied their trades.

In broad categoric terms, tea can be said to symbolize three aspects of Japanese thinking and living: relaxation, hospitality, and consolation. Stopping for a cup of tea means a breather in the activity of the day, for the very introduction of the steaming drink seems to spell relaxation. Housewives availing themselves of the services of carpenters and gardeners are obliged to offer tea and usually a light snack at ten in the morning and again at three in the afternoon. In offices, tea is served at the same times. Many companies hire girls who do little more than run errands, answer the telephone, and prepare tea in small pantries provided expressly for this purpose in all Japanese office buildings.

Nor do these girls serve tea only to the employees, since failing to offer a refreshing cup to all callers would be regarded as a serious breach of etiquette. Similarly, one is bound to offer a cup of tea——or nowadays something else roughly equivalent ——to any visitor who enters the living quarters of the house. (It is not required to refresh people who conclude their business in the entrance foyer.)

The cup of hot green tea can bring mental and spiritual help. For instance, brewed stronger than usual, it assists the intoxicated man to regain his senses. When people are in distress, their family or friends are likely to suggest a cup of tea as a spiritual palliative. In this last respect, the Japanese seem to put the kind of unquestioning faith in the soothing power of the cup of green tea that some Jews are traditionally said to have for the panacean virtues of the bowl of chicken soup.

Richard L. Gage

O-keikogoto, お稽古事

Practice or training, in the sense
of taking lessons.

Once I overheard a young girl talking to her friend on the
train. She said, "I'm twenty now so I must begin to study
ikebana." To the Western mind there is little connection between flower arrangement and the age of 20, but to the more
traditional-minded Japanese ikebana is one of the things that a
girl should study before she can become a suitable partner in
marriage. Other disciplines might include the tea ceremony,
cooking, dress-making, and perhaps the koto or piano. The only

Western equivalent to this might be the study of home economics but *o-keikogoto* has a uniqueness that is typically Japanese.

The uniqueness of o-keikogoto is centered not so much around the practical side of a wife's duties, such as cooking and sewing, but around the formal arts of ikebana and the tea ceremony; for it is in these studies that she may develop the frame of mind and sensitivity that is so in tune with the traditional sense of femininity. Just as the martial arts such as kendo and judo are believed to perfect the mind of the male; the more gentle arts of serving tea and arranging flowers may perfect the mind of the female. A Japanese woman is judged by her suitors not only for her physical beauty but also by her tender feelings, her grace, and delicacy. To the older generation these are qualities which can best be developed through these particular aesthetic disciplines.

The younger generation however has different feelings about o-keikogoto. For girls it has become just another thing that is expected of them. Actually there is not much a girl can do between the time she finishes her schooling and marriage except to attend the various schools which teach the feminine arts. She may of course graduate from a university but this may prove a liability in a land where a man's intelligence is taken for granted as being superior. For boys also it is not such a necessary prerequisite for marriage, although he will still look for the traditional sensitivity in a girl; personality and compatibility will probably be more important.

Japan is still a land where parents with traditional ideas control the marriage of their sons and daughters but Japan is changing rapidly. With this change we are already witnessing a change in the Japanese girl's personality. She is more relaxed and independent. This is good because now she may have an opportunity to broaden her scope of interest beyond the narrow limits of o-keikogoto. As for the arts themselves it would be better if they were studied by the truly dedicated regardless of sex.

Robert Wallace

Go, 碁

A game played with "stones"
on a squared board.

The ancestors of both chess and go were being played over four thousand years ago in India. Chess has spread to the East and West (it is known as *shôgi* in Japan), but go has until recently remained in Asia, even though it is an equally interesting, exciting, and even more complicated game.

It is, in fact, one of the most engrossing and challenging games ever invented. For businessmen playing during the lunch hour, go is an enjoyable pastime, like mahjong or cards. For the ardent amateur, it is intellectually an intensely demanding sport. But for the professional player, go is an art, and a serious one. Its philosophical ramifications have been investigated by many thinkers and writers from Confucius to Kawabata (who devoted a novel to the subject). Its scientific amplifications were defined when Einstein (who knew go) noted that: "The simpler the axioms the more difficult it becomes to find theorems in such a system."

If the rules of go are simple, the ways of playing the game are limitless. Theoretically its variations run up to an unimaginable number (10^{750}, or the number one followed by seven hundred fifty zeros), more than there are atoms in the universe. Yet only four axioms are needed to describe this game, and only one of them is not self-evident:

First, two players (black and white) alternatively put their stones on any unoccupied intersection of the nineteen by nineteen line roster board. Any stone thus placed may not be moved except when it is captured.

Second, if a stone or group of stones are completely surrounded by the enemy's stones, they are considered captured and are removed from the board.

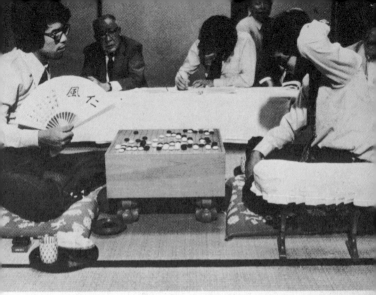

Title match: Ishida Shûhô (left) vs. Takemiya Masaki

Third, each prisoner or territory captured counts as one point.

Fourth, the situation called *kô*. If a configuration on a board is such that it would encourage the duplication of a play then this duplication is not allowed:

If, in the above, the white, marked ⊗, captures black, marked ⬤, black cannot then immediately recapture white, for this would mean duplication of the play.

This is, roughly speaking, really all you need to know to begin playing go. It is only after you have begun that the complications, wonders, and beauties of the game reveal themselves.

Manfred Wimmer

Pachinko, パチンコ

Pinball (originally onomatopoeic for
pachin, meaning "snap" or "click").

Pachinko is an upright pinball machine. Play is different now
from when the game appeared in Nagoya after the war, but it
remains simple. You buy steel balls, put them in a feeder tray,
and snap (pachinko) them up into the playing area using a
spring lever. The object is to win balls to trade in for prizes.

The game has always had tremendous popularity. While it is
perhaps the prime Japanese recreation, however, and is a thriving
business, its attraction escapes totally rational description. But it
fit the times perfectly when it was introduced. Japanese had
been freed from wartime dreariness, had much time, and wanted
an inexpensive recreation they could play alone in a colorful
setting.

More than colorful, the pachinko setting is noisy and gaudy.
Steel balls strike wood and glass and clatter into trays. Too,
today's machines light up and ring bells when they eject balls,
adding action and noise. Multiply it all by hundreds of machines and you get lots of living sound. There is also loud
background music, with the all-time favorite being the fast-paced
Imperial Navy March. Typically, moreover, pachinko joints have
low ceilings, poor ventilation, and a clientele of worker-types,
students, and good-for-nothings. *Yakuza* fought hard for pachinko
territories in the early days. O. Henry would surely have played.
Lautrec would have painted pachinko.

I think the noise and gaudiness contribute, but pachinko's
success comes largely from its machinations. Would you believe,
for example, that a *kugishi* ("nail" man) visits a joint every
night after closing in order to adjust certain key nails in each
machine? Also, the joint empties its machines at night and puts
in a new number of balls the next morning. During the day,
moreover, the number of balls inside a machine changes as
players either lose into it or win from it. The weight of the balls
can tip a machine just enough to affect the direction or bounce
of the balls. Professional players, many of them ex-kugishi,

adjust the reserve of balls in the feeder tray in order to offset the weight of the balls inside, thereby achieving the ideal nail bend. They "read" the nails and jockey the lever before they pachinko a single ball. Some pachinko parlors bar these men, for they can bankrupt a joint with one ball. Some kugishi and professionals have national reputations.

How accurately a player reads his machine and the adjustments he makes to pachinko his balls toward paydirt spell the difference between psychological elation and psychological despair. Pachinko's machinations keep you keyed high.

Thomas I. Elliott

Chanbara, ちゃんばら
Sword-play, as in drama and film.

If, like the song, you sometimes wonder "Whatever happened to Randolph Scott?" the answer is that the old-fashioned kind of action-filled morality for which he stood remains alive and well in Japan.

The *chanbara* is to Old Japan what the cowboy-and-Indian film was to the Old West. These Japanese Easterns, complete with a final slice-out, have so far managed to resist the changing tides of morality and retained their hold on the popular imagination. Though Gary Cooper and the ten-gallon hat have bit the dust, Mifune Toshirô and raked-up kimono are still in evidence.

Just as the morality of the Western was built upon an assumption that a man should be a man, and that the bad guy is always bad, so the chanbara has a traditional ethos worked into it.

Though just as simplistic as the American shoot-out, the Japanese carve-up is more complicated. John Wayne and Allan Ladd come into the lawless frontier town and dispense justice. Then they turn down the girl and walk out. Mifune Toshirô or the late Ichikawa Raizô have more of a problem. They are not free. Usually they are bound by ties of obligation to those above them. They have to choose between duty and inclination, between *giri* and *ninjô*, those great plot-movers of the chanbara, whether the vehicle be a low-budget TV series or a grand spectacle such as the Kabuki version of *The Loyal Forty-Seven Rônin*. They have to decide. Before the war they opted for duty; nowadays they side with inclination, with feeling——they save the girl and be damned to the *daimyô*.

Popular, simple-minded entertainment always means more than it says. American populist dreams were nourished on the Western and these in turn created more. A traditional Japanese dilemma finds expression in the chanbara. Because these forms are simplified, as are highly idealized models of life, they emphasize the values of society. Dreams tell a lot about a person; movies tell a lot about a society.

James R. Bowers

Janken, じゃんけん

Hand game, for purposes of tossing or elimination (alt. *jankenpon*).

Games that Japanese children play demand the deftness of a veteran craftsman and the quickness of a magician. In the game of *otedama*, for example, children juggle high into the air with either or both hands as many small, bean-filled sacks as possible. In the game of *ohajiki* they test their dexterity and control shooting marbles over tatami or the ground. And in origami, they fold flat, square pieces of paper into animals and other objects of amazing complexity.

Janken ("stone——paper——scissors") is perhaps the most popular of these children's games. It has a double function, however, for in addition to being a form of amusement, it serves as an arbiter as well. Instead of flipping a coin, people of all ages in Japan will decide an issue by simultaneously flinging forward their right hands and extending or curling fingers and thumb to represent the shape of stone or paper or scissors. A pair of scissors defeats a sheet of paper because scissors can cut paper. A stone defeats a pair of scissors because scissors cannot cut stone. But paper defeats stone because paper can be wrapped around stone.

Children playing janken as a game commonly use their left hands to keep score while making their right hands do the hard work. A child who wins first tucks in the thumb of his left hand. With each further victory, he tucks in finger after finger, from index to pinkie, making a fist; and if he keeps winning, his hand opens up like a fan, in reverse order, from pinkie to thumb. All the while, win or lose, his right hand is in perpetual motion, being continually flung forward in the shape of scissors or paper or stone.

According to one Japanese physiologist, the development of adroit hands and fingers has a very beneficial effect on the brain. If the cerebrum of the Japanese can be said to be particularly well developed, it is not because the Japanese were born that way, but rather because they engaged in pastimes

which demanded tremendous manual dexterity when they were young.

Watching Japanese children perform janken and other games with a mind-numbing nimbleness, I can only confirm the scholar's theory. And despite my stolid attempts to calculate the mathematical probabilities of a certain hand winning at any given moment, the little rascals beat me practically every time.

Edwin Fairbank

Manga, 漫　画
A cartoon or caricature; comics.

A widespread custom among young urban Japanese at present is the voracious reading of *manga*. This seemingly innocuous pastime is not, however, particularly noticed by visitors unless they happen to glance at an open magazine.

Though many of the comic-books are innocent enough, others share nothing with the world of *Donald Duck* or *Superman*. They abound with violence, with torture, with pain, with humiliation and degradation. The invariable sexual orientation abounds in sado-masochism, and suggests not that people use people for pleasure but that people use people for power. The outspoken violence one might expect here. The sick eroticism is something else.

Yet, it must mean something. The popularity of these publications is enormous and the magnitude of the industry is astonishing. Dai Nippon Printing Company at its Ichigaya, Tokyo branch, for example, utilizes thirty-four giant rotary presses twenty-four hours a day seven days a week to produce ten million manga weekly for Tokyo alone. Nor does one need statistics to see the extent of the mania. On the commuter trains those reading such publications far outnumber those reading newspapers, serious literature or technical books.

The question remains as to why the habit is so widespread. The Japanese admit the material is trash. The quality of the artwork is generally primitive. The humor is so low as to be in the "dirty joke" category. The whole genre is reminiscent of those adolescent fantasies we all experience at puberty. If you ask someone why he reads manga he will say, "Because they are easy reading." He doesn't want intellectual stimulation. He simply wants to be entertained in the most elemental fashion. Comics are a kind of vicarious catharisis——a controlled way of releasing the pressures bottled up in the darker recesses of the mind. Apparently it works. For the acts depicted in such lurid detail are rare in real life in Japan.

It is far too easy to criticize manga especially when one is influenced by Western standards of morality, and it may well be that manga do provide a useful social function. The very fact that they are so widely read while violent crimes are correspondingly infrequent at least merits investigation rather than condemnation.

James R. Bowers

Tachiyomi, 立ち読み
Reading (lit. "while standing")
in a bookstore.

In a nation with almost one hundred percent literacy and with perhaps the world's largest number and variety of weekly and monthly magazines, it is no wonder that the custom of *tachiyomi*——"standing reading," or bookstore browsing—— should be well entrenched, even in this age of television. The Japanese not only can read but do read, the gamut ranging from serious scholarship to political commentary to frivolous, gossipy "women's magazines" and comics.

The high tachiyomi tolerance of Japanese bookstore proprietors may be resignation to the inevitable on their part, but it is a godsend to ordinary citizens. What better way to kill time while waiting for a friend, a bus, or a train? One can beguile a free hour and at the same time survey the latest magazines or the new-book shelves both hardcover and paperback, since most bookstores carry both.

I frequently visit a well-stocked bookstore near my office during my lunch hour in order to browse, and it is invariably full of dozens of other people obviously doing exactly the same thing. In fact, the serious browsers, some of whom look well settled for a solid read, often make it almost impossible to move through the aisles.

One of the true joys of Tokyo for the tachiyomi addict—— especially for one without too much money——is the many small secondhand bookstores, which carry a hodgepodge of books and magazines of all kinds. In addition, there is an entire quarter in the downtown Kanda district filled with block after block of secondhand bookstores, many of them specialized.

It is interesting to speculate whether tachiyomi may not come fairly easily to the Japanese city dweller partly because people are accustomed to standing for long periods. First, there is the long standing on crowded commuter trains, often for an hour or more. Then the queuing for buses, and also outside theaters. There is also the custom of *tachigui*, "standing eating," at quick-order standup booths selling noodles or other traditional dishes — and now, of course, ice cream and hamburgers, too.

It may well be that another factor encouraging book-buying, and by extension tachiyomi, is the relatively underdeveloped and certainly underpublicized public-library system. People are word-oriented but seem not to be library-oriented. And somehow a library is a place one does not go to without a purpose; tachiyomi is free, easy, and requires no motivation at all.

Suzanne S. Trumbull

Shiken-jigoku,
試験地獄
Lit. "examination
hell," referring to
pre-entry school
exams.

Some years ago a student taking the entrance examination for
Sophia University turned in a blank paper, with none of the
questions answered. At the bottom of the empty page were
scribbled the words, "Dear Mother: I'm sorry." I thought of
those melancholy words again a few weeks ago as I watched this
year's crop of eager high school graduates packing the class-
rooms on our campus, laboring over the test papers which would
have such a strong impact on their futures. Multiply these
students, I thought, by the number of all the universities holding
entrance exams this year. Then add all the other middle school,
grade school and, yes, kindergarten pupils facing entrance exams
at this time of year in hopes of getting on the track to success

in university entrance exams. Add too the parents and teachers who suffer with their children or, in many cases, increase the suffering of their children for months and even years, leading up to this crucial juncture in a young person's life.

How many, I wondered, of this year's candidates taking exams all over Japan would end up writing "Dear Mother: I'm sorry" notes? How many would end up committing suicide? And even among the successful students, would there be any who would not be psychologically scarred by the heavy pressures of competition they had been subjected to for so long? Worse still, how many students would there be whose intellectual efforts were irrevocably channeled in mistaken directions because a whole education system has come to be focused on this kind of examination?

The expression "examination hell" is appropriate in many ways. Not only does the present system of exams cause torment to many people in various ways, but it suggests the Dantean image of a blazing inferno that is somehow out of control. No one knows how to go about correcting it. Since the Meiji era the Japanese have looked on university education as a sure means of upward mobility. And so with typical stoic acceptance, they take the entrance exam ordeal for granted and allow their lives to be affected to an amazing degree by their success or failure in that one single examination. The entrance exam has become an initiation rite assuming enormous importance to countless Japanese from their earliest childhood.

Perhaps initiation rites of some sort or other are useful in every culture. But there must be some other way of marking the passage to young adulthood that does not involve distorting a whole system of education. Watching the students undergoing this year's version of the annual ordeal, I thought of the "Dear Mother: I'm sorry" message, and it occurred to me that it would make more sense to write on every examination paper, "Dear Student: We're sorry." Signed: "All the people responsible for making your education system as mixed up as it is and who are not doing anything about trying to reform it."

William Currie

Kôkô-yakyû, 高校野球

High school baseball tournament.

Every year in August a sporting event takes place in Japan that is so popular that it sometimes causes a power blackout or brownout because so many millions of Japanese are watching it on television, resulting in circuit overloads. The same event also takes place in early spring but there is less danger of a power blackout because only the TV sets are on, not the air conditioners.

And what is this semiannual event that, for the Japanese, seems to be like the World Series, Rose Bowl game and World Cup combined? A baseball tournament. Not professional, not college, but high school. In America, the home of baseball, even the best high school baseball team would hardly be of interest to more than a few hundred local fans. Fifty thousand fans crowd into the Kôshien stadium near Osaka to watch Japan's best high school teams in action during the ten-day-long tournament. In addition a large part of the entire population of Japan follows every move on nationwide TV and radio coverage.

How can this enormous interest and enthusiasm be explained? From the player's point of view baseball seems to be the perfect sport for the Japanese. It is both a team sport and a sport in which most of the players can perform spectacularly as individuals and still help the team. The traditional sports of Japan, judo, kendo, sumo, etc., are individual sports rather than team sports. Most team sports require a cooperative or supportive effort by most of the team members and only a few of the players can be "stars." If a supportive member suddenly decides to be a "star" the team will usually suffer in consequence. Baseball is one exception to this characteristic of team sports. Team sports such as soccer, basketball, hockey, etc., do not interest the Japanese nearly to the same degree as baseball. The Japanese are particularly enthusiastic about individual sports such as golf, tennis, gymnastics, skiing, etc., and team sports which incorporate the capacity to satisfy the individual ego of every member of the team like baseball and volleyball.

From the spectator's point of view baseball also seems to be the ideal sport for the Japanese. The fans or supporters of each high school team are made up of the entire local community plus many others and they can identify enthusiastically with their team. And so baseball satisfies more than any other sport the needs of both player and fan in Japan and reaches its climax in the semiannual high school baseball tournament at Kôshien stadium.

The 34 teams (out of 2,709) that come to Kôshien as champions of their local areas play each other until the Japan championship is decided between the two remaining undefeated teams on the final day. These high school athletes receive nationwide attention and publicity.

Scouts from the professional leagues watch them closely. Some of the players step right into the Japanese big leagues. If one has the opportunity to see this tournament at Kôshien or on television it is not hard to understand why this sports event is by far the most popular one in Japan.

Albert W. Peterson

Neko, 猫
——Cat.

Though the Japanese are not notorious for their love of animals (as are, for example, the British) a special place seems to be set aside for the cat. As in most countries, it is believed to be a somewhat crafty beast; as in many, its independence is admired. In Japan, however, more of the feline qualities seem approved of. And it wasn't until I myself acquired a Japanese cat that I knew why. Now, I do. If the Englishman is a dog, if the American is a horse, if other countries are birds, wolves, marmosets——then, the Japanese is a cat.

I fell in love with her at first sight. She was perched on a pile of boxes outside a grocer's shop, and enticed me with a faint but coy meow. I was a bit drunk and sentimental that night in Yokohama, and I wobbled over to the boxes and tickled her affectionately under the chin. She climbed up my arm and onto my shoulder, and remained on her new perch until I reached home.

Even in my drunkenness, I feared that I had unwittingly made off with someone else's pet, little knowing at the time that unwanted kittens in Japan are commonly thrown out to take their chances as beggars in the wide, wide world rather than brutally drowned in a bucket of water. The kitten I had eloped with was no doubt one of these street scavengers. I fed kitty a saucer of milk and a fried egg, and bedded down with her for the night.

Returning home next evening from work and noting that she had not so much as sullied the sink even after being locked in the house for the whole day, I could not but marvel at her distinctly Japanese sense of self-restraint and purity. I was soon to marvel as well at kitty's sense of loyalty (she would meow incessantly whenever I had company until I let her in the room to join the party) and gratitude (she would catch cicadas and cockroaches and deposit their corpses on my pillow in the early hours of the morning as tribute).

Yet despite——or perhaps because of——her eccentric loyalty, kitty filled a great gap in my emotional life. She would share my bed every night without fail, sleeping with me cheek to cheek, her paws wrapped around my neck, and rousing me in the morning with gentle love bites and rough-tongued kisses.

Then, after a year of domestic bliss, I chanced to move to the capital city, and within a week the Tokyo traffic had struck her down. Though she managed to drag herself home, she died soon thereafter, on the veterinarian's operating table. Her ashes now lie in a Buddhist pet cemetery, not to prevent her ghost from becoming a lost and malevolent wanderer, but as a gesture of respect to her and her contribution to my emotional life.

Ian Gorman

Shinjû, 心　中

A double suicide; colloquially,
a lovers' suicide.

The practice of double-suicide for the purpose of preserving an emotional relationship, or bringing it to the ultimate to-getherness, by two people who, for social, political, or financial reasons, find it impossible to remain in a blissful state of unity by any other means, is known as *shinjû*.

It seems to have been particularly popular during the strict, feudalistic Tokugawa period owing to the almost incom-prehensibly ironclad controls that were imposed upon every con-ceivable aspect of life, with the death penalty or worse un-mercifully administered for even the slightest deviation from norms that no government in the world today would even dream of making laws about.

Shinjû was glorified as an art form in the plays of Chikamatsu Monzaemon (1653-1724). His shinjû plays were written for the Bunraku puppet theatre, where the performance by puppets probably served to take them a step further from reality than if they had been performed by human actors, which may provide a partial reason for the success of the extreme romanticization of grim reality at the time of their first presentation. In any case, their popularity was so great that they were soon adapted for presentation by live actors in the Kabuki theatre. And this popularity in these classical forms of theatre has not diminished even to this day, nor has their own general popularity, as witnessed by the numerous films and television dramas that have been based on these plays of Chikamatsu.

Even the practice of shinjû itself is still alive in Japan today. It manifests itself not only through pairs of lovers, but also when whole families find the sharing of death the only way they can preserve their unity and their mutual "face" or dignity against a hostile world.

Shinjû is just one more example of the fact that for centuries Japan has remained unchanging and unchangeable at heart, despite the surface of westernization and modernization. This kind of Japanese-ness defies value judgements——it simply *is*, and must be accepted in the context of the milieu that is Japan, if one wishes to gain an understanding of this land, its people and its culture.

Don Kenny

Kabuki performance of *Sonezaki Shinjū*, with actors Nakamura Ganjirō and Nakamura Senjaku

Kaimyô, 戒　名
Posthumous Buddhist name.

The postwar years have seen the number of practicing Buddhists in Japan decline to an ever smaller minority; yet by virtue of some past family affiliation, most Japanese continue to consider themselves at least nominal members of some sect. For the average family the question of religious practice is of little importance until one of its members departs this transient realm for the rewards of the next life: then, as funerals in Japan are invariably conducted according to Buddhist rites, it becomes necessary to engage a priest from the appropriate sect to read sutras before an altar set up in honor of the deceased and to prepare a suitable posthumous Buddhist name, or *kaimyô*, which will be inscribed on his tomb in addition to his secular name.

The granting of a kaimyô posthumously is a corruption of an earlier practice dating to the fourteenth century in which Buddhist names were given to adherents while still alive to serve as a guiding principle in their lives. A priest would be hard pressed to defend the modern practice, for there is little doctrinal support for it in the great body of Buddhist literature.

Nevertheless, bereaved families persist in demanding kaimyô and the temples continue to grant them. The tenacity of the custom is rooted in the manner in which kaimyô serve the interests of both priest and petitioner. For the temples, the granting of kaimyô represents a major source of income. Strictly speaking, kaimyô are not sold, but during a period of delicate negotiations both parties agree upon a "contribution," the amount of which is rarely specified and varies considerably with the prestige of the temple and the rank of the particular kaimyô in question. For the bereaved, too, the kaimyô is of no little importance, because family honor depends on the rank obtained for the deceased. Families feel bound to maintain at least the rank of kaimyô used by their forebears, and to improve upon it if possible.

While it is easy to criticize this sort of custom, one can just as

easily point out that many bereaved families elsewhere in the world will think nothing of spending enormous sums on a funeral. It seems that man cannot help coloring with a tinge of pride that awesome thing called death.

Eric M. Gordon von Hurst

Meinichi, 命 日

The anniversary of a death; the
deathday.

People in the West remember friends and family by celebrating birthdays or name days. In Japan, traditionally, observation of the day of decease, or *meinichi*, of relatives has served a similar function. Of course, in this case the one being remembered is not present to appreciate it. Or perhaps he is, in spirit. According to traditional popular Buddhist belief, departed ones maintain a karmic link with the living even across the barrier of death.

While the origins of the observance of meinichi may lie partly in the Chinese idea of ancestor veneration, imported to Japan along with Buddhism in the sixth century A.D., today meinichi does not necessarily carry predominantly religious connotations.

The primary function of the remembrance of a relative's death day is, it seems to me, in effect more often an opportunity for reaffirming the family solidarity of the living than it is a religious occasion commemorating the dead, even though on certain important anniversaries a Buddhist priest is called on to perform a memorial service. Basically, meinichi provides an opportunity——even an obligation——for family members to gather, thus serving to consolidate the sense of family identity.

The deceased are especially recalled on their meinichi. But rather than the living being drawn momentarily closer to the world of the dead, are not the dead temporarily returned to the realm of the living, insofar as they are revivified in the thoughts of those who survive them? Significantly, the word meinichi is written with two ideographs meaning "life" and "day." And in a sense, the remembrance of death days is indeed an affirmation of life and the living, as well as a guarantee of a measure of at least a kind of surrogate life following death.

Suzanne S. Trumbull

Jizô, 地 蔵

Buddhist guardian diety of
children (alt. *Jizô-bosatsu*).

Who is *Jizô*? Standard Western dictionaries and encyclopedias
are of no assistance whether one searches for the Japanese name
or the original Sanskrit, *Ksitigarbha*. Yet, though largely un-
known in other countries, he is ubiquitous in Japan.

You see him everywhere——in the city, in the country, at
crossroads, at temples. There he stands, carved in stone, bald,
hands folded or joined. Sometimes he has been given a red cloth
hood or bib; sometimes stones are neatly pyramided at his feet
or even on his head. He is a deity and mothers who have lost a
child thus send warm clothing for the small spirit; the stones are
needed to ford the icy rivers which separate this world from
paradise.

He appears in many forms. One of them is with six faces, the
Rokujizô, the faces corresponding to the six worlds of the
Buddhist creed. In his most common form, however, he appears
as an almost childlike priest, or an almost priestly child, standing
there to guide, to console.

His name is written with two ideographs——*ji* means "earth"
and *zô* may mean womb or bowels. The compound thus stands
for one whose womb was the earth itself. In the Latin of
Teilhard de Chardin, the concept of *mater terra* and *mater
materia* is close.

In English there is the saying, "from the womb to the tomb."
The Japanese might add to this, "and from the tomb to yet
another womb." For it is this continued life which Buddhism
traditionally promises. The waiting womb is thus, in a way, close
to that Christian paradise which is described as being "in
Abraham's bosom." And to guide one, there is this compas-
sionate and all-loving Jizô. When the gospel speaks of Jesus
being "moved to the depths of his being" at the sight of people
coming toward him like flocks without a shepherd, I feel something very Jizô-like in this emotion, this overflowing of pity and
of love.

Thus in the Jizô statues, in the nearby fields and the most remote mountains, I feel the force of Japanese religious feelings. Through this gentle deity they express their hopes for an all-pervading compassion, their inner need for peace and harmony.

Paul Rietsch

Maria Kannon,　マリア観音
Image of Kannon, worshipped as the
Virgin Mary.

One day in March 1865, only a few years after Japan had
opened her doors to the West following two and a half centuries
of isolation, a French missionary working at the newly-built
Ôura Cathedral in Nagasaki recorded in his diary:

I opened the church door and scarce had time to say
a Pater when three women knelt beside me and said
in low voices, placing their hands upon their hearts:
"The hearts of all of us do not differ from yours."

With these quiet words the presence of Christians in Japan
was revealed to the world. Although as many as 300,000 Japanese, mostly in Kyûshû, had been converted to the foreign faith
by the end of the 16th century by Jesuits, Franciscans, and
Dominicans from Europe, the feudal government, amidst rumors
of invasion directed by the "King of Rome" (i.e., the Pope),
grew suspicious of countrymen whose ultimate loyalty had
turned away from mortal masters and banned the religion. The
tempo of persecution and torture accelerated until not one
believer who remained alive dared to declare his faith in public.

Forced to choose between death and apostasy, many Japanese
Christians publicly recanted their beliefs while continuing to
worship privately, taking care that their service and objects of
worship would not arouse the authorities' suspicion. Believers
were aided by the fortuitous existence of the "White Kannon,"
the Buddhist goddess of mercy and patroness of women, said to
have the power of granting children to the faithful. The goddess
was normally depicted in seated position and holding a child——
a pose which lent itself to use as a surrogate Holy Virgin holding
the infant Jesus——and the underground Christians decorated
their home altars with statues of the goddess. To the curious
eyes of the authorities it was the "White Kannon"; but to the
faithful it was the "Maria Kannon."

The decision of the underground Christians, silent for seven
generations, to approach the French missionary was surely not

an easy one, for they had never in their own lifetime seen a foreign priest or a Catholic church. One of the three women asked to see an image of the Holy Virgin, and seeing that it held a child in its arms, she was satisfied that the Ôura Cathedral was the church of her ancestors.

Mary Helen Mine

Kurisumasu, クリスマス

Japanese pronun. of "Christmas."

While walking home one late December evening in Tokyo I heard the mellow strains of *Silent Night* drifting from a dimly lit schoolroom. A feeling of quiet joy welled in my breast as I listened to the soft refrain of this best-loved of carols, and I marveled that the Japanese would be celebrating Christmas as we do in Europe. When I strolled up to the window to catch a glimpse of the service, however, my joy turned into shock, for my eyes beheld a roomful of young couples waltzing to the music!

Every Japanese knows *kurisumasu*, the Japanese pronunciation of Christmas, but few feel about it in the same way that we do in the West. Christmas is a family affair in Switzerland, where I was born and raised, and we observed the birth of Christ quietly at home. In Japan Christmas is a much livelier occasion, often celebrated in some hotel banquet room where the music accompanies wining, dining and dancing rather than church services or family rites. By early December, street posters and newspaper ads publicize gala Christmas parties at most of the big hotels and boast extravagant dinners, a star-studded show, and Santa for the kids——for a price which makes one grateful that the season comes but once a year. All the tinsel and commercialism of plastic trees and decorated cakes seem strangely remote from the sweet-smelling, home-made cookies and sweeter-smelling, candle-lit evergreen trees I knew at home.

The Japanese have practically made a tradition of assimilating foreign customs, but complete assimilation has come only as a result of thorough adaptation of these customs into the indigenous culture. The Japanese think of Jesus as a saint like Buddha or Confucius——no more, no less——and, to the anniversary of Buddha's birth in the spring, Christmas provides a fitting winter complement. But it is not for me to criticize or complain; the Japanese have their own way of doing things which (even if those things are originally of foreign origin) no amount

of foreign influence will change. The caroling of *Silent Night* in Japan in circumstances rather more secular than those to which I am accustomed is perhaps one indication of what the Japanese have done to make Christmas their own.

Elizabeta Suzuki

Sho, 書

The art of calligraphy.

"All form emerges from nothingness, and to nothingness always returns." So teaches the Way, or Tao, from ancient times in China, and nowhere can this philosophy be experienced more directly than in *sho*, or Oriental calligraphy. It is so simple, no more than an elemental contrast between black ink and white paper; at the same time, it harbors a complexity that can never be fully explored in a lifetime. Much of the mystique surrounding things Oriental can be dispelled with time and familiarity,

but the mysterious fascination in the challenge offered by the brush and ink never seems to fade. If anything, its intensity mounts with the increasing ability of the person holding the brush to feel the forces that can move through pure line and form.

Black and white. According to the tradition passed down through thousands of years of Far Eastern art, these two are the embodiment of infinite possibility——the nothingness which is not "nothing" but the realm of endless potential from which forms define themselves and back into which they melt. Lao-tse taught that what we call black incorporates all colors; its use in sho endows the calligraphy with a universality denied by the expression of the same forms in any one color. If the characters were delineated in green the eye would be captured by the specificity of the green color and drawn away from the totality. Black and white have the power of eliciting the full rich universe.

Line and form and space comprise the visible elements of sho, and line defines the other two. Line is a living thing. Every single stroke is born where the brush meets the paper in the "brush awakening" (*kihitsu*), develops as the brush is "sent" on its journey (*sôhitsu*) and disappears with the "brush end" (*shûhitsu*) to the infinity from which it sprang. All of the individuality of that line is generated by the variations in pressure, angle of the brush, manipulation of the end hairs, direction, rhythms arising from placement of strokes within a character and of characters in an area and areas within the whole, rhythms of connecting strokes and so on. All are introduced during the instants of the line's creation through the personal rhythms of the individual wielding the brush. "A man and his sho are one and the same," we are told, and so closely do the movements of the brush mirror one's character and moods that I have often felt my teacher must know me as well as my best friend. But this is the most exciting part of it all, for you begin to discover that the responsive brush will reflect the subtlest inclinations or feelings that are you and you only, and you can give them life in black and white.

Sharon Ann Rhoads

Dô, 道
Lit. "path" or "way," with
philosophical connotations.

Sometimes it comes to seem a little silly, this notion of the *dô*, "the way," as the pursuit of a kind of truth or perfection. It did when, including a full-page picture, in a *fundoshi*, of Mishima Yukio, a book came out some years ago with the title *Taidô*, The Way of the Body, and so body-building was elevated to the level of a dô. Sometimes, too, it can seem unpleasant, as in the case of *bushidô*, which may have begun as a cult of loyalty, but which recently ended up as a cult of insane self-righteousness, the echoes of which we have detected in the behavior of certain young Japanese in certain Middle Eastern airports.

But it has been there at the center of things, one of the supporting pillars, for a very long time. People are always saying that the Japanese are not a religious people. Perhaps they are not, but they revere, as if sacred, certain guiding modes which would in most places be thought secular, and so the effect is much the same as if they were religious. It may be argued, indeed, that the absence of gods makes the religion more secure, because there is no one for the iconoclasts to decapitate. It is fairly easy to catch a god in error, but with a dô the most one can do is take it and see where it leads.

Mishima seemed to worry a great deal about the fact that young people had lost their reverence for the emperor. I too worry sometimes about a loss of reverence, but it is these less clearly focused sorts of reverence I worry about. The great curse of affluence, and few people would deny that Japan is an affluent country, is that nothing in all the stream of consumable products is very important, and so standards break down. Silly and unpleasant though it may sometimes seem, the dô has as its object of veneration the rigorous standard.

The idea that something is of all-consuming importance is the important thing, and the day when it disappears will be a day for lamenting and bolting the doors. There is no one more unhappy and more dangerous than the man who has everything and cares about nothing. The very notion of the dô is therefore such a reassuring one that we should not perhaps worry too much about its excesses. They are less frightening than its absence would be.

Edward G. Seidensticker

Yoin, 余 韻
A reverberation in the sense
of an overtone; resonance.

To a Japanese of average culture, the word *yoin* is very significant. Literally the word means reverberation, resonance —the sound a bell makes after being struck. Figuratively the word implies that something experienced stimulates the imagination and causes a positive memory to linger in the mind.

A situation in which a degree of transcendent experience is possible is said to contain yoin. A classmate, close friend, loved one, brother is going away, perhaps abroad, to war, to college, to prison for an extended period. Eyes meet, gleam, shy away. Words remain unspoken. An indelible memory is carried away by each. The fleeting smile which tells so much, the blush which answers many questions at once, the gentle touch of another at a particular moment, the silent reunion are thought of as situations containing yoin.

A friend once told me that Japanese people make little attempt to eliminate ambiguity from their speech. In fact a fair amount of illogical contradiction is preferred. He also made an example saying that if a situation exists which can be fully understood as a continuum ranging from one to ten, the average Japanese will explain the situation up to, perhaps, number six or seven and leave the remainder to the listener's imagination. An articulate Japanese of better than average culture will explain less, leaving more for the listener to grapple with.

Another friend recalled a movie which he considers an excellent example of yoin. The movie was made some years ago and is about a man suffering from a terminal disease. He determines to construct a park for children before his death. The last scene of the movie is of the man alone, sitting on a swing in the just-completed park. There is total silence except for the gentle sound of the metal-on-metal ticking of the swing. The camera closes in on the man and lumps come up into throats, eyes begin to glisten and noses begin to sting. Who can deny that this scene leaves one warm and choked up? Because of the skill of the camera work, the gentle, barely audible sound of the swing becomes, on the deep emotional level of the human experience, the thundering peal of a massive bell. The reverberations of this movie have continued these many years in my friend's memory, and his telling of it will remain in mine.

Walt J. Kleinedler

Yohaku,

余　白

Space (on painting) left
intentionally blank.

Sumi-e, by Shinoda Tôkô

The Japanese have a deeply ingrained sense of balance which can be observed throughout their culture ranging from art forms to expressions in daily life. Paradoxically the balance is not one of equality but of disparity. Objects of similar size and shape never oppose one another in a formal pattern and yet, by deliberate use, the element of emptiness negatively assumes a role akin to weight.

The essence of Japanese balance is found in the term *yohaku* ——literally "white space." Coined long ago, it referred to the background or untouched areas in ink painting. The elegance-in-proportion of the empty space in a given framework was admired as much as the brush strokes themselves. In old scroll painting, minimal suggestion was preferred to literal representation, thus allowing the viewer to participate in his mind's eye and complete the interpretation. Today the term yohaku is applied to new media, to color as well as black and white where solid areas play a dominant role. This principle of the use of space can be traced from the classics through modern art forms.

The deep-rooted Japanese preference for asymmetrical arrangement is not confined to graphic art but evolves naturally in small ways as well——the placement of food on a dish, the variety in size and shape of the dishes and even to the arrangement of the dishes themselves on the tray.

This intrinsic rule is the secret of the charm that can be observed in garden art from the diminutive bonsai arrangements to the classical landscape architecture of imperial palaces.

Those fascinating dimensions that make Japanese architecture unique also demonstrate numerous uses of off-balance spacing. Light is posed against dark on adjacent sides of a room as sliding translucent paper-covered doors offset the muted tones of remaining walls. Pattern is introduced to vary and to accent proportions in grid-work, in exposed beams, in the edging of floor mats and in wood grains. Windows are never standardized in shape or placement. Usually they are designed more as openings for receiving light than for viewing the exterior and may appear as horizontal strips at floor level, as vertical shafts at the side of an alcove, and occasionally in the shape of a fruit or flower at the end of a hallway. Furnishing and decor is kept at a minimum to allow enjoyment of the beauty and restraint of basic spacing.

Opposing nature's rules of random inequality, man alone balances equals, one against the other. Yet obvious equality in balance stimulates a sense of competitiveness. When yohaku or empty space is combined with broken space, a sense of restfulness can result. One looks not only at trees and leaves themselves but at the shapes and areas of sky they enclose, not only at the distribution of stones on a beach, but the water and sand between. The Japanese respect for nature herself was probably the basis for their rules of spacial relationship.

Frances Blakemore

CONTRIBUTORS

Ronald V. Bell, born in New Jersey in 1931, is the editor of *The Japan Experience.* Resident of Japan for the past twenty years, he lives in Tokyo and is a consultant and free-lance writer.

Frances Blakemore, born in America, is author of *Who's Who in Modern Japanese Prints,* and directs the Franell Gallery in Tokyo. Also an artist of wide repute, she has had a number of one-man shows.

James R. Bowers, born in South Carolina in 1945, is president of the Eiffle Language Center in Tokyo.

Richard J. Bowring, born in England in 1947, attended the graduate school of the University of Tokyo.

Holloway Brown, born in America, is Associate Professor of Journalism and Director of Public Information at the International Christian University.

Angela Carter, born in England in 1940, is a well-known novelist. Among her books are *Several Perceptions* and *Heroes and Villains.* She lived in Japan from 1969 to 1971 and also during 1974.

Jean-René Cholley, born in France in 1940, Visiting Professor in the Foreign Languages Department of the Aichi Prefectural University.

Thomas J. Cogan, born in Ohio in 1947, doctoral candidate in Japanese literature at the University of Hawaii.

Jane Alexandra Corddry, born in Massachusetts in 1950, in Japan for the second time, studying Japanese theater.

William Currie, born in Philadelphia in 1935, former Dean of the International College, is now teaching Japanese literature at Sophia University.

Glenn Davis, born in Texas in 1946, has been in Japan for the past fifteen years. At present he is a lecturer at Tôyô University.

Katharine L. Day, born in New York in 1949, is the author of a number of English education books for the Modern English Institute.

Fred Dunbar, a Japanese citizen, was born in 1916, and pursued his academic career at the University of Cambridge. At present he is a free-lance writer in Japan.

Thomas I. Elliott, born in America in 1931, is the translator of numerous books, essays and articles on the business world, and editor of various publications.

Earle Ernst, born in America in 1911, is the leading foreign authority on Kabuki. Author of *The Kabuki Theater*, he is at present professor emeritus at the University of Hawaii.

Edwin Fairbank, born in America, is a specialist in Japanese history. At present he works as a translator and writer in Tokyo.

Masako Ford, born in Japan, is married to an American and currently makes her home in Illinois, with her husband and two children.

Edward Fowler, born in America in 1947, is a specialist in Japanese literature, having received his master's degree in that discipline from the University of Michigan.

Bernard Frank, born in France in 1927, is a graduate of the University of Paris. Professor at the Ecole Pratique des Hautes Etudes.

Richard L. Gage, born in America in 1934, has been in Japan since 1964. He is a well-known editor and translator.

Frank Gibney, born in Pennsylvania in 1924, is one of the best-known writers on Japan. His latest book is *Japan: The Fragile Superpower*.

Ian Gorman, born in England in 1942, has lived in Japan for the last five years. He is at present a free-lance journalist.

Daniel L. Gossman, born in South Dakota in 1942, has been in Japan since 1968. At present he is with International Telephone and Telegraph, Inc., in Tokyo.

Charles Hancock, born in America, graduated from both Boston College and Georgetown University. Lecturer at Sophia University.

Jean-Pierre Hauchecorne, born in France in 1908, is a graduate of Paris University. Professor of French at Kyoto Foreign Languages University.

John Herrick, born in Indiana in 1942, news editor for NHK's Radio Japan in Tokyo.

William F. M. Horsley, born in 1949, a producer of English language programs, as a part of the BBC's continuing affiliation with NHK's Radio Japan.

Richard J. Hugel, born in Chicago in 1936, Vice President and Director of Studies at English House, Ltd., in Tokyo.

Eric M. Gordon von Hurst, born in 1939 in California, tenured lecturer at Tôyô University and a research criminologist.

Guy Jean, born in America but raised in Europe and Japan, is a student of comparative cultures and is at present a free-lance writer in Tokyo.

Donald Keene, born in New York in 1922, is a well-known author, translator, editor, lecturer, and teacher. Among his many books is *Living Japan*. At present he is Professor of Japanese at Columbia University.

Don Kenny, born in Kansas in 1936, has been in Japan since 1959. He is the author of *A Guide to Kyogen* and founder of the Don Kenny Kyogen Players.

Walt J. Kleinedler, born in America in 1944, English instructor at the Sacred Heart Girls' High School.

Stephen Kohl, born in Nebraska in 1944, director of the Japan Study Center at Waseda University in Tokyo.

Domenico Lagana, born in 1925, is an Argentinean who graduated from Buenos Aires University in 1955. At present he is a free-lance writer in Tokyo.

Joseph Lapenta, born in New York in 1941, is an adept of the Ikenobô school of ikebana and at present works with the Time-Life Language Center in Tokyo.

Wood-hung Lee, born in Canton in 1952, is at present majoring in the Japanese language at the Tokyo Foreign Languages University.

Sally Lynne McCreary, born in America in 1945, has been in Japan studying pottery in both Kyoto and Tokyo.

Mary Helen Mine, born in Indiana in 1944, a graduate of Harvard University, is at present with Sophia University.

Shirley Miyasaki, born in America in 1950, presently studies art history, and is with the Executive Institute for Foreign Languages.

Anne Elizabeth Murase, American, born in 1948, is an instructor of cultural anthropology at Sophia University, and has published papers on related subjects.

Walter Nichols, American, born in 1919 in Tokyo, and member of the American foreign service, is at present president of Nichols Enterprises, Inc.

Mareile Onodera, born in Germany in 1943, is an artist of repute and has held many one-man shows.

Albert W. Peterson, American, associate professor in the English Department of the School of Education at Waseda University in Tokyo.

Sharon Ann Rhoads, born in Washington, D.C. in 1944, has translated many books, including *Her Place in the Sun*. In addition she has written many articles on Japan.

Paul Richards, born in America in 1925, has been in and out of Japan for many years. At present he works for a Tokyo publishing house.

Donald Richie, born in Ohio in 1924, the well-known film critic, is the author of many books on Japan including *The Inland Sea*. He continues to live and write in Tokyo.

Mary Evans Richie, American, lived in Japan from 1957 to 1966. She has written of her experiences in her first novel, *A Romantic Education*.

Paul Rietsch, born in France in 1912, has been in Japan since 1948. Author of several books on Japan, he is head of the French Department at Sophia University.

Jack Rucinski, born in 1944 in Wisconsin, with the East/Western Center at Waseda University. He is the author of papers and articles on Japanese literature.

Alfred Scholz, born in Germany in 1928, is a foreign judo expert who teaches and writes about this sport.

Edward G. Seidensticker, born in America in 1921, is a well-known translator and teacher. Author of *Kafu the·Scribbler* and the translator of *The Tale of Genji.*

Elizabeta Suzuki, born in Switzerland in 1944, was educated in Europe before coming to Japan where she married and continues to live.

Norman H. Tolman, American, served with the American foreign service and at present runs the Tolman Collection with his wife, Mary.

Suzanne S. Trumbull, American, studied Japanese literature at Columbia University, has lived in Japan a total of twenty years, and is at present an editor.

Cihákováa Vlasta, born in Czechoslovakia in 1944, is at present a free-lance art critic.

Thomas Walker, born in 1942 in North Carolina, is at present with the PL Gaigo Gakuin in Tokyo.

Robert Wallace, born in America in 1943, has been in Japan for the past ten years. He is at present with the Kanda Gaigo Gakuin.

Jack Walraven, born in Canada, graduate of the University of British Columbia, is at present director of the Kanda Gaigo Gakuin.

Meredith Weatherby, born in Texas in 1915, is well-known as the translator of two of Mishima Yukio's finest novels. He is president and editor-in-chief of John Weatherhill, Inc.

Manfred Wimmer, born in Austria in 1944, has published extensively on *go* and is at present German instructor at both the Tamagawa and the Shôwa Yakka universities.

INDEX